CREATION

CREATION

A Witness to the Wonder of God

MARK D. FUTATO

P&R
PUBLISHING
P.O. BOX 817 • PHILLIPSBURG • NEW JERSEY 08865-0817

Unless otherwise indicated, all Scripture quotations are from the HOLY BIBLE, NEW INTERNATIONAL VERSION®. NIV®. Copyright © 1973, 1978, 1984 by International Bible Society. Used by permission of Zondervan Publishing House. All rights reserved. Italics in Bible quotations indicate emphasis added.

"God, All Nature Sings Thy Glory" Taken from *Hymns II.* © David Clowney, assigned to InterVarsity Christian Fellowship. Used by permission of InterVarsity Press, P.O. Box 1400, Downers Grove, IL 60515. *www.ivpress.com*

"Vast the Immensity" © Edmund P. Clowney. Used by permission.

Page design by Tobias Design
Typesetting by Michelle Feaster

Printed in the United States of America

Library of Congress Cataloging-in-Publication Data

Futato, Mark David.
      Creation : a witness to the wonder of God / Mark D. Futato.
          p.   cm.
      ISBN 0-87552-203-3 (pbk.)
      1. Creation. 2. God—Attributes. I. Title.

 BT695 .F88 2000
 231'.4—dc21

                                                    00-021179

To my dear friend
Don Chartrand.
If everybody loved and understood
God's creation as you do,
what a different world
this would be.

Contents

Preface

Creation: A Witness to the Wonder of God was written while I lived in the majesty of California's mountains and valleys, deserts and beaches. As I type these words in the lushness of central Florida, I can look out my office window into the pines, oaks, and palmettos, where I enjoy watching the likes of deer, pileated woodpeckers, a great horned owl, osprey, and an eastern fox squirrel, just to mention a few of the marvelous creatures that make this area their home.

This book was originally a series of sermons that were a sheer delight to prepare and to preach. It has been an equally delightful experience to transform those sermons into chapters for a book. One of my deep passions in life is experiencing God in his creation. Whether on a beach in southern California or in an electrical storm in central Florida, I can sing, "In the rustling grass I hear him pass, he speaks to me everywhere," because creation is a witness to the wonder of God.

As this book will show, the wonder of God can been seen throughout the tapestry of creation. I have the privilege of seeing some of the most exquisite threads of this tapestry in the face of my wife, Adele. I am grateful to God for the beauty of her person and to her for the beauty of her contribution to me and to this project. The idea to publish this material came from Adele. The book was her idea, and so was the first step in the process, as she transcribed the sermons from their original audio form. Because of her impetus I am sharing with you *Creation: A Witness to the Wonder of God*. Adele also contributed to the substance of the book by her many editorial suggestions. Adele herself is a witness to the wonder of God.

Many thanks also go to Mike Rutherford, a former student of mine, who worked his editorial magic on the manuscript at an early stage. It was a pleasure working with Mike to transform oral sermons into written prose. Mike's theological insights have also enhanced the book.

I am grateful to Bryce Craig at P&R Publishing for his willingness to accept the manuscript for publication and to Thom Notaro and freelance editor Jim Scott, whose editorial expertise transformed a draft into a finished product. The staff at P&R has been a delight to work with.

My own passion for God and his creation has been greatly stirred by my friend, Don Chartrand. Don's passion is contagious. And my hope is that through your reading of this book, you too will catch that passion. May the Spirit of the risen Lord Jesus fill you with wonder as you experience the wonder of God in *Creation*.

Chapter One

Witness to the Glory of God

The heavens declare the glory of God;
*   the skies proclaim the work of his hands.*
Day after day they pour forth speech;
*   night after night they display knowledge.*
There is no speech or language
*   where their voice is not heard.*
Their voice goes out into all the earth,
*   their words to the ends of the world.*
*   (Ps. 19:1–4)*

The glory of God is a phrase familiar to Christians, and Psalm 19:1 contains the familiar words, "The heavens declare the glory of God." But what does *glory* mean, and how do the heavens declare God's glory? And if "the whole earth is full of [God's] glory" (Isa. 6:3), why does David focus our attention on the heavens? Are they the grandest display of the glory of God? This chapter will provide biblical answers to these and related questions.

WHAT IS MEANT BY *THE* GLORY OF GOD?

We use the word *glory* with reference to God in at least
two ways. When we say we are doing something for the glory
of God, we use the word *glory* with reference to the superla-
tive honor that is due to God. Such honor is in view in verses
like 1 Samuel 2:30: "Those who honor me I will honor." But
this meaning of *glory* is not the primary one in Scripture,
nor is it the sense that we will be looking at in this chapter.

Glory also refers to something similar to an attribute or
virtue of God, to what theologians call his "perfections."
While glory is not technically an attribute, a certain glory
does belong exclusively to God because of the manifestation
of his perfections. Because he is perfect, he is glorious. This
is the glory in view when David says that "the heavens declare the glory of God." But just what is it that the heavens
are declaring?

A Common Misunderstanding

First, let's eliminate a common misunderstanding of the
glory of God. The Hebrew word for *glory* is *kavod,* which is
related to words meaning "heavy" or "weighty." Therefore,
many writers explain God's glory as his weightiness or significance. And, of course, we use the English words *heavy*
and *weighty* to indicate significance, don't we? We say,
"That's a heavy problem you're dealing with," or, "Those are
weighty issues you're facing." What do we mean by *heavy* and
weighty? We mean that something is important, significant,
or serious.

Perhaps you have heard or read that God's *glory* refers to
the truth that God is weighty or important, that he must be
taken seriously, that his character is one of significance. I
don't want to deny that God is weighty in this sense. He certainly is. He is the most significant person with whom we

have to deal. But the Old Testament doesn't use the word *kavod* in connection with God being weighty.

This is an important point because the way the biblical writers use a word determines its meaning in the Bible, not the way we use it in our twentieth-century culture. Let me give you an example. Has anyone ever said that you are nice? If so, you probably took it as a compliment. Well, the word *nice* comes from the Latin word *nescius,* which to the early Romans meant "ignorant." Now how do you feel? Before you try to track down your friend, remember that today we don't use the word *nice* to mean "ignorant." Who is using the word must be taken into consideration when determining its meaning. Similarly, the meaning of *glory* must be determined by how the writers of the Hebrew Bible use the word *kavod.*

So what do they mean when they speak of God's glory? They are referring to the visible manifestation of God's radiant splendor.

God's Glory Is Visible

When *kavod* is used of God's glory, it means, first and foremost, something that is visible. You perceive his glory with your senses, and in particular with your sense of sight.

God's Glory Is Seen on Mount Sinai. In the Old Testament, the Israelites—the descendants of Abraham, Isaac, and Jacob—lived in Egypt for some four hundred years. Having been reduced to slavery, they cried out to God, and he brought them out of Egypt "by a mighty hand and an outstretched arm" through his servant Moses (Deut. 4:34). God led the Israelites into the Sinai Desert and to Mount Sinai, where he made a covenant with them.

When God made this covenant with Israel on Mount Sinai, he displayed his glory. The Israelites experienced this glory with their senses, in particular with their sense of sight. Look at what Moses says in Deuteronomy 5:22–24:

> These are the commandments the LORD proclaimed in a loud voice to your whole assembly there on the mountain from out of the fire, the cloud and the deep darkness; and he added nothing more. Then he wrote them on two stone tablets and gave them to me. When you heard the voice out of the darkness, while the mountain was ablaze with fire, all the leading men of your tribes and your elders came to me. And you said, "The LORD our God has *shown us his glory* and his majesty, and we have heard his voice from the fire. Today we have seen that a man can live even if God speaks with him."

Israel was *shown* the glory of God (v. 24). She *saw* that glory in the deep darkness and in the blazing fire (vv. 23–24). God's glory is *visible,* and it was seen on Mount Sinai.

God's Glory Is Seen at the Cleft in the Rock. Soon after God made a covenant with Israel on Mount Sinai, Israel broke that covenant by making a golden calf (Ex. 32), which probably was an idolatrous representation of the true God. After God judged these people, he commanded them to continue their trek to the Promised Land without his presence (Ex. 33:1–4). But Moses persuaded the Lord to go with Israel (vv. 15–17). Moses then made the ultimate request, "Now show me your glory" (v. 18). The Lord responded,

> "I will cause all my goodness to pass in front of you, and I will proclaim my name, the LORD, in your presence. I will have mercy on whom I will have mercy, and I will have compassion on whom I will have com-

passion. But," he said, "you cannot *see* my face, for no one may *see* me and live." Then the LORD said, "There is a place near me where you may stand on a rock. When my glory passes by, I will put you in a cleft in the rock and cover you with my hand until I have passed by. Then I will remove my hand and you will *see* my back; but my face must not be *seen.* " (vv. 19–23)

Moses asked to see God's glory. God said, in effect, "OK. But I'm going to put you in a cleft in the rock, and when my glory passes by—that is to say, when I pass by, because my glory is simply a visible manifestation of my own radiant splendor—I'm going to have to cover you with my hand. For if you were to look straight into my glorious face, you wouldn't be able to live. But after my glory has passed by, I'll remove my hand and let you see my back—that is, I'll give you a glimpse, a small glimpse, of my glory. You can see a little bit of my glory, but you could never endure seeing the fullness of my glory." God's glory is *visible,* and Moses saw it at the cleft in the rock.

God's Glory Is Seen at the Dedication of the Temple. While the Israelites were living in the wilderness, God gave them instructions for building the tabernacle, a beautiful tent where God's special presence would be experienced by his people (Ex. 25–31). Years later, King David expressed his desire to build God a permanent dwelling, a temple (2 Sam. 7). God, however, gave this task to David's son, Solomon.

After Solomon finished building the temple, he assembled the elders, priests, and Levites to dedicate it (1 Kings 8:1–5). The setting into place of the ark of the covenant (the quintessential symbol of God's presence with his people) into the Most Holy Place was central to this dedication ceremony (vv. 6–9). Then, "when the priests withdrew from the Holy Place, the cloud filled the temple of the Lord. And the priests could not perform their service because of the cloud, for the glory of the Lord filled his temple" (vv. 10–11).

Both the cloud and the glory filled the temple, for the cloud was the visible manifestation, the perceptible manifestation, of the glory of God. And such was the radiance of the glory that the priests couldn't stay in the temple—just as Moses couldn't see the face of God and live. When the glory cloud filled the temple, the priests had to leave. God's glory is *visible,* and it was seen at the dedication of the temple.

God's Glory Is Radiant

God's glory is not just visible, but also radiant—filled with bright, shining light—as we have already begun to see. Many things are visible, but not everything that is visible is also radiant.

The Radiant Face of Moses. After Moses saw the glory of God from the cleft in the rock, he came down from Mount Sinai with the two stone tablets of the Ten Commandments in hand (Ex. 34:29). Moses did not realize that his own face was now glowing. God had shown his back to Moses—just a small portion of his glory. Because Moses had seen that glory, his own face reflected the radiant glory of God. Exactly how his face radiated, no one is sure, but there was some physical radiance that could be hidden with a veil (see 2 Cor. 3:13).

I once radiated in a similar way—not that I saw the glory of God as Moses did! When I was candidating for the position of professor of Old Testament at Westminster Seminary in California, I had interviews on Thursday and Friday, but had Saturday off, before I was to preach on Sunday. So what do you do when you are in southern California for the first time? Well, you go to Sea World! It was in the early spring, and in Washington, D.C., where I lived at the time, nobody worried about sunburn in early spring. So off I went to spend Saturday at Sea World. By Sunday morning, my face was glowing! My fair-skinned forehead was shining brilliant red. I had encountered the radiance of the sun. My forehead was reflecting, as it were, the radiance of the sun.

My experience provides a rough analogy to that of Moses. He encountered the radiant glory of God, and when he came away from that encounter, his face was radiating.

The Radiant Vision of Ezekiel. For Ezekiel, the "heavens were opened" and he "saw visions of God" (Ezek. 1:1). An examination of Ezekiel's vision makes it clear that he saw the radiant glory of God. Note the accent on the perceptible, the visible, and the radiant:

> I looked, and I *saw* a windstorm coming out of the north—an immense *cloud* with *flashing lightning* and surrounded by *brilliant light.* The center of the *fire* looked like *glowing metal.* (v. 4)

> The appearance of the living creatures was like *burning coals of fire* or like *torches. Fire* moved back and forth among the creatures; it was *bright,* and *lightning flashed* out of it. (v. 13)

> Spread out above the heads of the living creatures was what looked like an expanse, *sparkling* like ice, and awesome. (v. 22)

> Above the expanse over their heads was what looked like a throne of *sapphire,* and high above on the

throne was a figure like that of a man. I saw that
from what appeared to be his waist up he looked like
glowing metal, as if full of *fire,* and that from there
down he looked like *fire;* and *brilliant light* sur-
rounded him. Like the *appearance* of a rainbow in the
clouds on a rainy day, so was the *radiance* around him
(vv. 26–28a).

What did Ezekiel see in all of this radiance? "This was the appearance of the likeness of the glory of the LORD" (v. 28b).

Now look again at Psalm 19:1, "The heavens declare the
glory of God." What David is telling us is that the heavens
are a visible manifestation of God's radiant splendor.

How Do the Heavens
Declare the Glory of God?

There are a variety of ways in which the heavens declare
God's glory. Let's dig a little deeper into Psalm 19 to find
out what some of them are.

To Look at Creation Is to Look at the Glory of God

Creation in general is the visible manifestation of God's
radiant splendor. Notice the structure of verse 1:

| The heavens | declare | the glory of God; |
| the skies | proclaim | the work of his hands. |

This verse illustrates a poetic device called parallelism. Parallelism is the corresponding of two clauses or phrases,
where the second one usually adds to the first. "The heavens" corresponds to "the skies," "declare" corresponds to
"proclaim," and "the glory of God" corresponds to "the

work of his hands." "The work of his hands" is the creation in general (see Ps. 104:31 in context) and adds specificity or further definition to "the glory of God." By means of parallelism, Psalm 19:1 teaches us that the creation is a manifestation of the glory of God.

So when Isaiah sees the Lord high and exalted, seated on his throne (Isa. 6), he also hears the angels singing, "Holy, holy, holy is the LORD Almighty; the whole earth is full of his glory" (v. 3). The angels are saying that all of creation displays the radiant splendor of God. Therefore, to look at creation is to look at the glory of God.

The Heavens Play a Particular Role in Declaring God's Glory

Psalm 19:1 also teaches us that the heavens play a particular role in declaring the glory of God in at least two ways. First, the heavens are seen every day. Second, they are seen everywhere. Let's take a look at these two truths.

The Heavens Are Seen Every Day. The heavens play a special role in declaring the glory of God because they appear daily. Verse 2 begins, "Day after day they pour forth speech." Day after day the brilliant sun is radiating. *Radiant* describes the sun well, because it shines so brightly that no one can stare at it for long. Day after day the radiant sun is manifesting the radiant glory of God. (Keep in mind that in Israel, where David composed this psalm, cloudy days are the exception, not the rule.)

Verse 2 continues, "Night after night they display knowledge." Night after night the stars are radiating, too. The most recent estimate of the number of stars that can be seen with the most sophisticated telescope is ten to the twenty-third power. That is 100,000,000,000,000,000,000,000 stars! Mind-boggling!

Why did God create so many stars, all of them out there radiating light? Because it takes 10^{23} radiating stars just to begin to approximate his radiant glory.

Then there is the moon, shining night after night. The moon doesn't radiate its own light, just as Moses' face didn't radiate its own light. The moon reflects the light that comes from the brilliant sun. What an analogy for the whole of creation: just as the moon does not radiate its own light, but the light of something else, so the whole creation—and the heavens in particular—radiates the glory of God, a glory that comes from outside the creation, from the Creator himself.

The Heavens Are Seen Everywhere. The heavens also play a special role in declaring the glory of God because they can be seen everywhere. Verses 3–4 record, "There is no speech or language where their voice is not heard. Their voice goes out into all the earth, their words to the ends of the world." Wherever you find people on the face of the earth, the heavens are there declaring the glory of God.

This is why the apostle Paul says in Romans 1 that everybody knows the reality of the true and living God, the Creator of heaven and earth. Everybody everywhere sees the sky, the sun, the moon, and the stars, which all bear witness to the glory of God. This declaration of God's glory reaches the most remote part of the earth. If you could somehow find the place on the earth that is the farthest away from all civilization, right there would be a clear declaration of the glory of God. In fact, the irony is that the farther away you get from civilization, the grander is the display of the glory of God, at least at night. Let me explain.

Once my sons and I were camping in the Cuyamaca Mountains of southern California at an altitude of about five thousand feet. One night we decided to enjoy the stars. So we moved away from the campfire, where a good bit of ground light lessened our view of the stars. It was magnificent to look up and see the grand sweep of the Milky Way, to gaze upon the glory of God!

The farther you move from ground light, the more majestic is the vista. I have a friend who used to fly an F-14 in the Navy. He tells of flying off an aircraft carrier in the middle of the ocean, climbing to forty thousand feet, turning off all the interior lights, and looking up at the myriad shining stars. I can't imagine what he saw, but I know he saw the radiant splendor of the glory of God.

The heavens play a particular role in declaring the glory of God, because they are seen every day and everywhere.

IS THERE A GREATER MANIFESTATION OF THE GLORY OF GOD?

As you read Psalm 19 in the context of the book of Psalms, and also in the context of the whole Bible, you are driven to ask, Is there a yet greater manifestation of God's glory than what we see in the heavens? The answer is yes!

God's Glory Transcends the Heavens

To transcend means "to go beyond the limits" of something. In writing about the glory of God, I am writing about something that ultimately transcends, or goes beyond the limits of, my understanding. God's glory also transcends the limits of the heavens.

In Psalm 8, David writes, "O LORD, our Lord, how majestic is your name in all the earth!" (v. 1a). He continues, "You have set your glory above the heavens" (v. 1b). What he means is that while the heavens declare the glory of God, they do not exhaust that glory. There is a glory of God that is "above the heavens," that transcends them.

Another psalm echoes this theme: "The LORD is exalted over all the nations, his glory above the heavens" (Ps. 113:4). What is this transcendent glory, this glory that is greater than that which fills the heavens?

Jesus Christ, the Greater Glory

God's glory in creation finds its supreme manifestation in Jesus Christ. But the eternal Son of God is also the divine Creator, so how can God's glory in creation be manifested in the Creator? The answer lies in the Incarnation: the Creator became the creature. In Christ, deity took on the form of humanity. In Jesus Christ, the Creator and the creature meet, and the glory of the Creator is manifested in the creation.

Jesus Is the Image of the Invisible God. The apostle Paul tells us that Jesus Christ is "the image of the invisible God" (Col. 1:15). God is invisible, and therefore we cannot see him. But Jesus is his image. When we look at Jesus as he is described in the pages of Scripture, we see the invisible God. Do you find that hard to believe? The author of the book of Hebrews says the same thing. In Hebrews 1:4 he writes that Jesus, the Son, is "the exact representation" of the Father's being. Do you want to see the exact likeness of God? Then look at Jesus Christ as he is revealed in the Bible. Jesus Christ is the image of the invisible God.

Jesus Is the Ultimate Manifestation of the Glory of God. Jesus Christ is the ultimate manifestation of God's radiant splendor. Hebrews 1:3 says, "The Son is the radiance of God's glory." The radiant glory of the Father is found in the Son. The Son is the radiance of God's glory, the manifestation of that glory. And Jesus displays God's radiant splendor repeatedly in Scripture. He displays it in his incarnation, in his transfiguration, and in his exaltation.

Jesus Displays God's Radiant Splendor in His Incarnation. "The Word became flesh and made his dwelling among us. We have *seen his glory*" (John 1:14). One result of the eternal Son of God becoming a man was that people saw the glory of God displayed before their very own eyes. They saw God's holiness in Jesus' sinless life, his power in the miracles that Jesus performed, and his love in Jesus' self-sacrificial life.

Jesus Displays God's Radiant Splendor in His Transfiguration. "After six days Jesus took with him Peter, James and John the brother of James, and led them up a high mountain by themselves" (Matt. 17:1). This ascent up a high mountain echoes Moses' ascent up Mount Sinai. "There he was transfigured before them" (v. 2a). To be "transfigured" means that "his face shone like the sun, and his clothes became as white as the light" (v. 2b). That is very similar to what Moses' face looked like when he came down from the mountain. Jesus' face shining like the sun is also reminiscent of the shining figure of the man in Ezekiel's vision.

Matthew continues: "While he was still speaking, a bright cloud enveloped them" (v. 5a). The bright cloud recalls both the cloud on Mount Sinai and the cloud of glory that filled the temple.

The Old Testament is full of pictures of the glory of God, including the glory on Mount Sinai, the glory cloud that filled the temple, and the glory in chapter 1 of Ezekiel. But none of these pictures can hold a candle to the reality: the glory of God in the person of Jesus Christ.

Jesus Displays God's Radiant Splendor in His Exaltation. The apostle John writes,

> I turned around to see the voice that was speaking to me. And when I turned I saw seven golden lampstands, and among the lampstands was someone "like a son of man" . . . with a golden sash around his chest. His head and hair were white like wool, as white as snow, and his eyes were like blazing fire. His feet were like bronze glowing in a furnace. . . . His face was like the sun shining in all its brilliance. (Rev. 1:12–16)

In this passage John recounts a vision he had of Jesus roughly sixty years after Jesus had ascended to heaven. Here John piles up one shining image after another to describe Jesus, because the glory of God in Christ shines most brilliantly in the exalted Christ, who has returned to the glory he had with the Father before the world began. This is the glory that Jesus had promised he would reenter (John 13:32) and had prayed that he would reenter (John 17:5).

Yes, the heavens manifest the radiant splendor of the true and living God. But the heavens in all their glory pale in comparison to the glory of God manifested in the person and work of Jesus Christ.

WHAT ARE SOME IMPLICATIONS FOR CHRISTIANS IN THE THIRD MILLENNIUM?

What difference can these truths make? I trust that as you think about, meditate on, and ponder the truth that God's glory is reflected in his world and in his Son, God himself will give you insight—your own insight—into how this truth can impact *your* life. Let me share with you a few of the insights that I have received through my study of God's Word.

No One Has an Excuse for Failing to Worship the True and Living God

In Romans 1, Paul teaches us several things. He says that because of their fallen nature, people ascribe the glory they see in the creation to idols rather than to the true and living God. "Although they claimed to be wise, they became fools and exchanged the glory of the immortal God for images made to look like mortal man and birds and animals and reptiles" (vv. 22–23). People see the glory of God in creation, but then they make the fundamental mistake of failing to distinguish the Creator from the creation. They see the glory of God in created things and say, "We must worship them." When they respond to the glory of God with worship, they are on the right track. But when they worship and serve the creation rather than the Creator, they err greatly.

All of us, by nature, tend to ascribe the glory we see to created things—what the Bible calls idols—rather than to the Creator. Because of our fallen nature, we try to suppress, reduce, and even eliminate the truth of God's glory, and then obliterate any reminder that we are not God. "The wrath of God is being revealed from heaven against all the godlessness and wickedness of men who suppress the truth by their wickedness" (v. 18). Every one of us sees the glory of God, but we don't want to acknowledge the true and living God, because by nature we are hostile to God, unwilling and unable to submit our lives to him (Rom. 8:7). And so, by all sorts of means, we suppress that truth.

But that is impossible. God's invisible qualities are clearly seen in creation, "since what may be known about God is plain to them, because God has made it plain to them. For since the creation of the world God's invisible qualities—his eternal power and divine nature—have been clearly seen, being understood from what has been made, so that men are without excuse" (1:19–20).

When you talk to neighbors, coworkers, or relatives who say there is no God, you can be sure they know better. They know that there is a God, but they are suppressing the truth they know—and they know that too. They are doing everything they can to suppress the truth that God is there. When you are talking to people, you know this about them: God has told them that he is there. He is not silent.

No person on earth has a legitimate excuse for not worshiping the true and living God. We all have a revelation of his invisible qualities. His glory is evident to everyone, everywhere, every day.

You Can Fully See the Glory of God in Creation Only Through Faith in Jesus Christ

Now, I am not saying that you have to be a Christian to see the glory of God; I am not contradicting all I have said up to this point. Rather, I am saying that to *fully* see the glory of God, you must have faith in Christ.

In 2 Corinthians 3, Paul contrasts the fading glory of the old covenant with the surpassing glory of the new covenant, which is manifest in the person of Jesus Christ. To make the contrast, he takes us back to the aftermath of Moses' view of God from the cleft in the rock. In verses 12–16, Paul says,

> Since we have such a hope, we are very bold. We are not like Moses, who would put a veil over his face to keep the Israelites from gazing at it while the radiance was fading away. But their minds were made dull, for to this day the same veil remains when the old covenant is read. It has not been removed, because only in Christ is it taken away. Even to this day when Moses is read, a veil covers their hearts. But whenever anyone turns to the Lord, the veil is taken away.

The full truth of the glory of God is veiled to people who are without the Spirit of Christ. It is only when they are united to Christ that the veil is removed so that people can begin to see the glory of God in its fullness. Then they begin to praise God for his glory rather than suppressing the truth of that glory. The denial of his glory is increasingly replaced by the confession of his glory. At the heart of Christianity is the call to cease worshiping and serving the creation, and to ascribe all of the glory of the creation to the Creator.

In verse 16, Paul affirms that "whenever anyone turns to the Lord, the veil is taken away." You see, we all have sinned and fallen short of the glory of God. We have failed to manifest in our lives the excellence of God's character. We have failed to reflect the excellence of his holiness, justice, righteousness, and wisdom. Yet we who have come to faith in Christ by God's grace are now being transformed more and more into the likeness of that glory. As verse 18 teaches, "We, who with unveiled faces all reflect the Lord's glory, are being transformed into his likeness with ever-increasing glory, which comes from the Lord, who is the Spirit." We are becoming more like him and are increasingly able to reflect his excellent character.

Just as Moses' face shone when he encountered the glory of God, so we are shining more and more as we come and worship God, as we study his Word, and as we gaze upon the glory of God in creation. In every aspect of our lives, we are increasingly able to radiate the glory of the invisible God. We reflect God's glory more and more as we become more and more like Christ in our thoughts, our words, and our deeds.

We see the glory of Christ in his perfect life. Have you ever lied? Christ never did. That is just one manifestation of the perfection of Christ's life. And we must have that perfection in order to have a right relationship with God. So, by faith, we receive the perfect righteousness of Christ.

But, in particular, we see the glory of Christ in an unexpected place—on the cross. In John 17:5, Jesus says, "And now, Father, glorify me in your presence with the glory I had with you before the world began." God glorified the Son in particular on the cross. We have fallen short of the glory of God, and the wages of our sin is death. When Christ was on the cross, he paid the penalty for our sins and broke the power of sin in our lives, so that, through faith in him, we would be declared righteous by God and be transformed more and more into the glorious likeness of Christ.

You Can Develop New Eyes to See the Glory of God in Creation

Psalm 119:18 says, "Open my eyes that I may see wonderful things in your law." We could adapt this verse like this: "Open my eyes that I may see wonderful things in your world." This is not to say that God's revelation in creation and in the Bible are the same thing or that they are on the same level. The revelation in creation and the revelation in the Bible both need to be interpreted, but the revelation in the Bible takes precedence in at least two ways: (1) the Bible alone teaches us how to be reconciled with God, so that we will no longer suppress the truth revealed to us in creation, and (2) the Bible teaches us how to interpret the revelation in creation correctly. We do, however, need to see the importance of the revelation in creation, and we need God's Spirit to help us read that revelation correctly. Thus, for example, children can know that their science lessons are important and related to their faith. God wants them to study science and to enjoy it, because as they do, they are learning about the true and living God who created their world.

Young people who are thinking about careers are free to consider a career in science. John Calvin has a beautiful quotation that describes the privilege scientists have because their vocation enables them to gaze more clearly at the glory of God in creation. He writes,

> There are innumerable evidences both in heaven and on earth that declare his wonderful wisdom; not only those more recondite matters for the closer observation of which astronomy, medicine, and all natural science are intended, but also those which thrust themselves upon the sight of even the most untutored and ignorant persons, so that they cannot open their eyes without being compelled to witness them. . . . To be sure, there is need of art and of more exacting toil in order to investigate the motion of the stars, to determine their assigned stations, to measure their intervals, to note their properties. As God's providence shows itself more explicitly when one observes these, so the mind must rise to a somewhat higher level to look upon his glory. (*Institutes of the Christian Religion*, Library of Christian Classics, 20 [Philadelphia: Westminster Press, 1960], 1.5.2)

We need more people with a biblical worldview engaging in the sciences in our day. We all have the privilege of studying God's revelation in creation. And the more we know about the creation, the more we see the glory of God.

You Can Join the Heavens in Declaring the Glory of God

If the heavens, without intellect, without voice, without spirit, declare the glory of God day after day, how much more may we do it, since we are created in God's image. A good way to begin is by meditating on the words of David Clowney's hymn, "God, All Nature Sings Thy Glory":

> God, all nature sings thy glory, and thy works pro-
> claim thy might;
> Ordered vastness in the heavens, ordered course
> of day and night;
> Beauty in the changing seasons, beauty in the
> storming sea;
> All the changing moods of nature praise the
> changeless Trinity.

> Clearer still we see thy hand in man whom thou
> hast made for thee;
> Ruler of creation's glory, image of thy majesty.
> Music, art, the fruitful garden, all the labor of his
> days,
> Are the calling of his Maker to the harvest feast of
> praise.

> But our sins have spoiled thine image; nature,
> conscience only serve
> As unceasing, grim reminders of the wrath which
> we deserve.
> Yet thy grace and saving mercy in thy Word of
> truth revealed
> Claim thy praise of all who know thee, in the
> blood of Jesus sealed.

> God of glory, power, mercy, all creation praises
> thee;
> We, thy creatures, would adore thee now and
> through eternity.

Saved to magnify thy goodness, grant us strength
to do thy will;
With our acts as with our voices thy commandments to fulfill.

QUESTIONS FOR PERSONAL REFLECTION OR GROUP DISCUSSION

1. Where have you seen the glory of God in creation most brilliantly displayed? How did you feel?
2. Do you know people who say they don't believe in God? Have you ever talked with them about God? How might creation serve as a point of contact in your relationship with them?
3. Is your heart moved to worship as you are out and about in God's creation? Why do you think you respond as you do?

Chapter Two

Witness to the Power of God

I pray also that the eyes of your heart may be enlightened in order that you may know the hope to which he has called you, the riches of his glorious inheritance in the saints, and his incomparably great power for us who believe. That power is like the working of his mighty strength, which he exerted in Christ when he raised him from the dead and seated him at his right hand in the heavenly realms, far above all rule and authority, power and dominion, and every title that can be given, not only in the present age but also in the one to come. (Eph. 1:18–21)

What do you pray for? Stop and think about two or three things you pray for frequently. What are they?

Is the word *power* on your list? Do you pray frequently for power? When the apostle Paul prayed for the church at Ephesus, he prayed "that the eyes of your heart may be enlightened in order that you may know . . . his incomparably great *power*" (Eph. 1:19). When Paul prayed for Christians, one item high on his list was power: that they might know God's

23

incomparably great power—not only that they might know *about* that power, but also that they might know *the reality* of that power in day-to-day living. In this chapter we will consider creation as a witness to the power of God.

When Paul tells us in Romans 1:18–20 that creation testifies to the reality of God, one of the two characteristics of God that he mentions is power.

> For since the creation of the world God's invisible qualities—his eternal *power* and divine nature—have been clearly seen, being understood from what has been made, so that men are without excuse. (v. 20)

GOD'S POWER EXERTED IN CREATION

Let's consider first how God's power was and is exerted in creation. We will discover that his power was and is exerted in creation and providence—in his bringing the universe into existence and in his continual sustaining of the creation.

In Bringing the Universe into Existence

> But God made the earth by his power;
>   he founded the world by his wisdom
>   and stretched out the heavens by his under-
>   standing. (Jer. 10:12)

> Ah, Sovereign LORD, you have made the heavens
> and the earth by your great power and outstretched
> arm. Nothing is too hard for you. (Jer. 32:17)

The Bible testifies to the fact that when God brought the universe into existence, he exerted a tremendous amount of power. Scripture provides many examples of the power that God exerted at creation, but one in particular has fascinated me since I was a boy. I have always been fascinated by the geological process of mountain building. This process is referred to in the great creation hymn, Psalm 104:

> You fixed the earth on its foundations;
>> not to be moved forever.
> With the ocean, as with a garment, you covered it;
>> above the mountains the waters stood.
> At your rebuke they fled,
>> at the sound of your thunder they took to
>>> flight;
> as the mountains rose,
>> they went down the valleys,
>> to the place you had fixed for them.
> You set a limit they may not pass;
>> nor shall they cover the earth again.
>> (vv. 5–9 NAB)

This psalm describes the beginning of creation, when water covered the earth and no mountains could be seen. As the mountains rose up out of the waters, the waters ran down into valleys to form oceans.

What kind of power did it take to make the mountains rise? Once, when referring to this text in a sermon, I tried to lift the pulpit from the floor to provide an example. Although it was not an extremely large pulpit, I was unable to lift it. Can you imagine how much power it would take to lift a mountain?

What kind of power did it take to make the mountains rise? Perhaps you have seen large mountains like the Rocky Mountains. They are a huge block of granite that was at one time below sea level, and then, inch by inch, was lifted up fourteen thousand feet. Imagine what enormous power it took to do that!

I have flown into the Denver airport numerous times. When you look east as you fly in, the earth seems to be as flat as a pancake. But when you look west, you see this huge block of granite rising up to the sky. How much power was exerted to raise those large mountains? The words from a familiar hymn provide the answer: "I sing th'almighty pow'r of God that made the mountains rise" (Isaac Watts). God's power was exerted at creation in bringing the universe into existence.

In Sustaining the Universe

> The LORD reigns, he is robed in majesty;
>   the LORD is robed in majesty
>   and is armed with strength.
> The world is firmly established;
>   it cannot be moved. (Ps. 93:1)

When Psalm 93 says that "the world is firmly established; it cannot be moved," it is referring not only to the initial establishing of the creation, but also to the ongoing, day-to-day sustaining of the "natural processes" in creation—all of which is accomplished by God's great strength.

> The Son is the radiance of God's glory and the exact representation of his being, sustaining all things by his powerful word. After he had provided purification for sins, he sat down at the right hand of the Majesty in heaven. (Heb. 1:3)

God the Son exerts his power day by day, moment by moment, to maintain, to sustain, all of the processes on our earth and in the whole universe.

An illustration of this power in the ongoing processes of creation dates back to May 18, 1980, at Mount St. Helens in Washington. When the power of God was exerted at the eruption of this volcano, ashes and debris were spread over an area of 150 square miles. Before the eruption, the elevation of Mount St. Helens was 9,677 feet. Afterwards, it had fallen to 8,364 feet. That's a 1,313-foot drop in elevation! Now that's earth-moving power! Can you imagine the bulldozer it would take to move 1,313 feet of soil that fast and spread it over 150 square miles? Such is the power of God to maintain the processes of creation each and every moment.

"I sing th'almighty pow'r of God that made the mountains rise, that spread the flowing seas abroad and built the lofty skies." God's power is mightily exerted in creation.

GOD'S POWER DISPLAYED IN CREATION

Since God brought the creation into existence and now sustains it by his great power, we can see that power displayed in various ways.

If you live in the Midwest, you probably think of tornadoes. If you're from California, earthquakes probably come to mind. Floridians think of hurricanes. All of these are manifestations of God's great power. Although the Bible frequently mentions stormy winds and earthquakes as signs of God's power, it focuses our attention on the sky as the chief manifestation of it.

> Sing to God, O kingdoms of the earth,
>   sing praise to the Lord, *Selah*
> to him who rides the ancient skies above,
>   who thunders with mighty voice.

Proclaim the power of God,
>   whose majesty is over Israel,
>   *whose power is in the skies.*
You are awesome, O God, in your sanctuary;
>   the God of Israel gives power and strength to
>   his people.
Praise be to God! (Ps. 68:32–35)

"Proclaim the power of God . . . whose power is in the skies." In some special way, God's power is displayed in the skies. When the psalmist says, "You are awesome, O God, in your sanctuary," he is referring to God's power in the skies, since the sanctuary in view is the heavenly sanctuary, as is clear from Psalm 150:1, "Praise the LORD. Praise God in his sanctuary; praise him in his mighty heavens." In this verse, "in his sanctuary" is further described as "in his mighty heavens." So his sanctuary here is not Solomon's earthly sanctuary, but the Lord's heavenly sanctuary. "His mighty heavens" are literally "the firmament of his power," "the heavens of his power," the place where his power is gloriously displayed. There are two places where God's power is displayed in the skies—in the stars and in storms.

God's Power Displayed in the Stars
There is an amazing declaration in Psalm 147:4–5:

He determines the number of the stars
>   and calls them each by name.
Great is our Lord and mighty in power;
>   his understanding has no limit.

God's ability to determine the number of the stars and call them each by name is a manifestation of his power. Yet, the psalmist could see only several thousand stars with his naked eye.

Let's think about the stars for a moment. Consider our nearest star, the sun. Imagine the largest nuclear reactor on earth and the power that it can generate. The sun is really a big nuclear reactor, apparently using fusion instead of fission to generate power.

How big is this solar reactor? It is so large that you could put a million of earth's nuclear reactors in it. Well, actually, it is much bigger than that. It is so large that you could put one million of our earths in it! That's a mind-boggling reactor, generating mind-boggling power. And, of course, what boggles the mind even more is the fact that our sun is just average as stars go. And it is only one star in our galaxy, the Milky Way.

Think about our galaxy. A galaxy is a cluster of stars. In God's governing of the universe, stars cluster together into galaxies. Have you ever looked up on a clear night to gaze upon the Milky Way? According to one estimate, two hundred billion nuclear generators are out there in our galaxy.

But our galaxy is only part of a cluster of galaxies. Just as stars cluster together in galaxies, so galaxies cluster together with other galaxies. Our galaxy is only one of twenty galaxies in a cluster called the Local Cluster, which in turn is part of a super cluster, of which there are many in the whole universe.

How many nuclear power plants are out there? As we said in chapter 1, there are estimated to be 100,000,000,000,000,000,000,000 power-generating stars in the universe!

The psalmist says that God "determines the number of the stars and calls them each by name." No wonder he goes on in the very next verse to say, "Great is our Lord, and mighty in power." If the psalmist, who could only see several thousand stars with the naked eye, stood in awe of the power of God in the skies, how much more can we?

God's Power Displayed in Electrical Storms

Psalm 29 is a description of a powerful electrical storm—the kind experienced in central Florida or in the high Sierra:

> Ascribe to the LORD, O mighty ones,
> > ascribe to the LORD glory and strength.
> Ascribe to the LORD the glory due his name;
> > worship the LORD in the splendor of his holiness.
> The voice of the LORD is over the waters;
> > the God of glory thunders,
> > the LORD thunders over the mighty waters.
> The voice of the LORD is powerful;
> > the voice of the LORD is majestic.
> The voice of the LORD breaks the cedars;
> > the LORD breaks in pieces the cedars of
> > > Lebanon.
> He makes Lebanon skip like a calf,
> > Sirion like a young wild ox.
> The voice of the LORD strikes
> > with flashes of lightning.
> The voice of the LORD shakes the desert;
> > the LORD shakes the Desert of Kadesh.
> The voice of the LORD twists the oaks
> > and strips the forests bare.
> And in his temple all cry, "Glory!"
> The LORD sits enthroned over the flood;
> > the LORD is enthroned as King forever.
> The LORD gives strength to his people;
> > the LORD blesses his people with peace.

Verses 1 and 2 exhort worshipers to ascribe to the Lord glory and strength. When we experience a certain power, we are to say, "That power belongs to the Lord."

Now, where is this power displayed, this power that we are to ascribe to the Lord? Verses 3–9 tell us that the power of God is experienced in a good, old-fashioned electrical storm.

The Power of God in Thunder. Note the focus on thunder in verse 3:

> The voice of the LORD is over the waters;
>> the God of glory thunders,
>> the LORD thunders over the mighty waters.

The "voice" of the Lord is a metaphorical description of thunder. The Hebrew word translated "voice" is the word *qol* (pronounced like *coal*), and *qol* is somewhat onomatopoeic, sounding like a rumble of thunder. The word *qol* rolls through the psalm as thunder rolls across the land. As one reads the psalm in Hebrew, one hears the thunder rolling through the psalm itself. The psalmist draws our attention to the power of thunder in verse 4:

> The voice of the LORD is powerful;
>> the voice of the LORD is majestic.

And in verses 5–6 he shows just how powerful the Lord's thunderous voice is:

> The voice of the LORD breaks the cedars;
>> the LORD breaks in pieces the cedars of
>> Lebanon.
> He makes Lebanon skip like a calf,
>> Sirion like a young wild ox.

God's power is enough to break stately cedars, enough to make the mountains move like a calf skipping across a field.

Have you ever been in an electrical storm and felt the ground shaking under your feet? Why is it that little children, when they hear a crack of thunder, come running to mom and jump on her lap? The power of God is being displayed. How many children have been told that thunder is God speaking? Exactly! One biblical metaphor for thunder is God's "voice."

Of course, you do not have thunder if you do not first have lightning, because thunder is simply the result of air being heated so rapidly that it expands with a gigantic boom as it breaks the sound barrier. So the psalmist also focuses our attention on the power of lightning.

The Power of God in Lightning. The psalmist describes lightning in verses 7–8:

> The voice of the LORD strikes
> with flashes of lightning.
> The voice of the LORD shakes the desert;
> the LORD shakes the Desert of Kadesh.

If the ancient psalmist stood in awe of God because of lightning, we can do so all the more in the twentieth century, given how much more we know about lightning. At this particular moment, there are an estimated 3,500 electrical storms going on throughout the world. These electrical storms are producing more than 100 bolts of lightning per second, 6,000 per minute, 360,000 per hour, 8,640,000 per day, 259,200,000 per month, and 3,153,600,000 per year! And each bolt carries approximately 25,000 volts of electricity per inch. That is a lot of electrical power!

Where is all this power coming from? The Bible answers:

> See how he scatters his lightning about him,
> bathing the depths of the sea. . . .

He fills his hands with lightning
  and commands it to strike its mark.
      (Job 36:30, 32)

He unleashes his lightning beneath the whole
      heaven
  and sends it to the ends of the earth. . . .
He loads the clouds with moisture;
  he scatters his lightning through them.
      (Job 37:3, 11)

Do you send the lightning bolts on their way?
  Do they report to you, "Here we are"?
      (Job 38:35)

If there is all of this power in lightning, there must be some greater Power behind the lightning. Psalm 29 begins by saying, "Ascribe to the LORD . . . strength." When you see power in creation, you are to ascribe that power to the Lord in worship.

By commanding us to ascribe the power in creation to God, Psalm 29 forbids us to ascribe it to some impersonal natural process or to nature itself. How wrongheaded it is for us to encounter the power of God and then ascribe it to an impersonal force. The psalmist tells us to give God the glory and ascribe that power to him in worship.

Many people in our culture have a faulty view of creation, and they worship the creation rather than the Creator. That is certainly wrong. But, it is also right, to a certain extent. That is, when such folks see the glory and power of God in creation, their hearts are constrained to worship. They worship the creature rather than the Creator, but at least they worship.

How is it for those of us who claim to believe in a Creator, but who have accepted naturalistic explanations of life? Are our hearts inclined to worship the true and living God when we see his power displayed in the stars, in electrical storms, and in all sorts of other ways? The answer too often is no. We are to remind ourselves regularly to ascribe that power to the true and living God and worship him.

But even more dramatic than the power displayed in the stars and in the storms is the power of God manifested in the resurrection of Jesus Christ from the dead.

The Power of God in the Resurrection of Jesus Christ

Incomparably Great Power. In Ephesians 1:19, Paul prays that we may know God's "incomparably great power." What does "incomparably great" mean? It means that we cannot ultimately compare God's power to anything else. All the power of all the stars and all the storms does not even begin to compare with the true power of God, for his power knows no limit. God has only used the tip of his little finger in exerting all of that power.

So, if God's power is incomparable, why am I trying to compare it to this or that? Well, because Paul does. He tells us that God's power cannot be compared to anything, and then he adds, "That power is like . . ." (v. 19). Paul is willing to compare God's incomparably great power to something. What is God's incomparably great power like? It's "like the working of his mighty strength" (v. 19)—not just his strength, but his mighty strength—"which he exerted in Christ when he raised him from the dead" (v. 20).

The resurrection of Jesus Christ from the dead, then, is the grandest display of God's power. In it, God breathed life into the dead body of Christ. God took that body entombed in darkness and brought it into the light of life. God took that cold body and warmed it with the light of life. In the resurrection of Christ, God did what none of us could ever do: he conquered the power of death, the awesome power of death.

And death really is powerful, isn't it? The book of Ecclesiastes says, "No man has power over the wind to contain it; so no one has power over the day of his death" (Eccl. 8:8). Medical technology can go a long way in putting off death. In all likelihood, if it were not for medical intervention, two of my four children would not be alive today. Medical intervention is wonderful in what it can do to save life. But medical technology cannot put off the inevitable forever. It cannot ultimately resist the day of one's death. Death, that hideous power that awaits each of us, is the penalty for our sins. All die because all have sinned and fallen short of the glory of God. No one has power over death—except God.

God alone has power over death. He has absolute power over it. As Hannah sang, "The LORD brings death and makes alive; he brings down to the grave and raises up" (1 Sam. 2:6).

I would not dare to write about the power of God if I knew only that his power was incomparably great. What sinner could endure the power of a holy and angry God? We can contemplate the power of God with joy and wonder only because we know two things: that God is powerful, and that *God is loving*. His love is so great that he sent his Son to live a life of perfect obedience in our place and to die on the cross to pay the penalty for our sins. His power is so great that he raised his Son from the dead, that we might have everlasting life. His power is not against us. His power is for us, because he has loved us in his Son.

Incomparably Great Power for Us. More amazing than Paul's comparison of God's incomparably great power is the affirmation that this power is reserved "for us who believe" (Eph. 1:19). God's power is not always exercised *for* people. It is at times exercised *against* them. The Bible testifies to

God's use of lightning to destroy his enemies, of earthquakes to swallow up unbelievers, of his power to bring judgment and to exercise justice (see chapter 5). The most amazing thing is that we who deserve death and destruction by the power of God can escape through that very same power. God's power is not arrayed against us; it is arrayed for us, because he has loved us in Christ.

> One thing God has spoken,
>   two things have I heard:
> that you, O God, are strong,
>   and that you, O Lord, are loving.
>   (Ps. 62:11–12)

GOD'S POWER EXERCISED FOR US

We come to the final point of this chapter: God's power is exercised for us. Jeremiah prayed,

> Ah, Sovereign LORD, you have made the heavens
> and the earth by your great power and outstretched
> arm. Nothing is too hard for you. (Jer. 32:17)

Jeremiah's logic is that if God had the power to create the universe, then there is nothing in the universe that is too difficult for him to do. God has the power to do whatever he wishes, and he wishes to use his power for us in a variety of ways. Let me just mention a few of the ways in which God uses his power for us.

God Uses His Power to Strengthen Us

Psalm 29, which we have already looked at, begins by exhorting us to "ascribe to the LORD glory and strength" (v. 1).

The psalm focuses on the power of God in electrical storms (vv. 3–9). It concludes, "The LORD gives strength to his people" (v. 11). What is the appropriate response to God's display of power in creation? Two appropriate responses are to ascribe that power to the true and living God and to believe that God will provide the necessary strength for Christian living.

Now consider Psalm 68:34–35:

> Proclaim the power of God,
>> whose majesty is over Israel,
>> whose power is in the skies.
> You are awesome, O God, in your sanctuary;
>> the God of Israel *gives power and strength to his*
>> *people.*
> Praise be to God!

Do you see the same logic here? Knowing about God's power in the skies provides you with confidence that God has the power to strengthen you in your walk with him. Do you pray for this power? Do you depend on this power?

Are there sins that you have not yet overcome? Do you need power to overcome them? Have you given up and resigned yourself to the continued presence of these sins? Have you quit the fight and decided to tolerate certain sins? Do you believe there is no way for you to overcome them? Have you despaired?

Look at the creation to find hope in the Creator. Look to the testimony within his world. The next time you are tempted by the thought that the power you need is just not there, think of the creation and the power of God manifested in it—in the stars, in the lightning, in the earthquakes, in the hurricanes, in the tornadoes—and remember that that power, especially the power of Christ raised from the dead, is God's power for you to draw on to overcome the sin that remains.

Where in particular do you need strength? Ask God to share his power with you for the conquest of whatever sin remains in your life. God exercises his power to strengthen us.

God's Power Exercised to Sustain Us

Recall the words of the psalmist:

He determines the number of the stars
    and calls them each by name.
Great is our Lord and mighty in power;
    his understanding has no limit.
The LORD sustains the humble
    but casts the wicked to the ground.
        (Ps. 147:4–6)

Our God is mighty in power. He is mighty enough to determine the number of the stars and to name each one. And he is mighty enough to sustain you, as you humbly depend on him.

Again I quote Psalm 68:34–35:

Proclaim the power of God,
    whose majesty is over Israel,
    whose power is in the skies.
You are awesome, O God, in your sanctuary;
    the God of Israel gives power and strength to
        his people.
Praise be to God!

Just several verses earlier, David says,

Summon your power, O God;
    show us your strength, O God, as you have
        done before. (v. 28)

And just a few verses prior to that we read,

> Praise be to the Lord, to God our Savior,
>   *who daily bears our burdens.* (v. 19)

Do you have burdens? Do you have sorrows? Are there situations in your life that at times weigh heavily upon you? Do you sometimes wonder if you have the strength that it takes to endure another day? From time to time we all experience the burdens that come from living in a world of sin and its misery. Life can be burdensome.

The book of Proverbs says, "Each heart knows its own bitterness" (Prov. 14:10). You and you alone know the weight of your burdens. Your spouse, your children, your parents, your friends—nobody really knows your heartache. Each person alone knows the weight of his or her own burdens in life.

"Nobody knows the trouble I've seen. Nobody knows, but Jesus." Jesus not only knows your trouble, but also has the power to sustain you when life's burdens grow great. Sometimes you cry out with the psalmist,

> *Sustain me* according to your promise, and I will
>   live;
>   do not let my hopes be dashed. (Ps. 119:116)

And when you cry out, God answers you with these words:

> My hand will *sustain him;*
>   surely my arm will *strengthen him.* (Ps. 89:21)

So I say to you as you read this book,

> Cast your cares on the LORD
>   and *he will sustain you;*
>   he will never let the righteous fall. (Ps. 55:22)

God's Power Exercised to Save Us

God has power to strengthen us, to sustain us, and to save us. Again, in the now familiar Psalm 68, we read,

> Our God is a God who saves;
>> from the Sovereign LORD comes escape from
>> death. (v. 20)

God has the power to save us from the sin that remains in our lives. He has the power to save us from eternal death. He has the power to raise us up on the Last Day. This power to save is seen throughout the creation because the Savior is the Creator. The power of the Creator is the power of the Savior.

If you want to know how much power God has to save, just look at his power in creation. The Creator and the Savior are one. Most gloriously we see the power of the Creator when he raised Jesus Christ our Savior from the dead.

My prayer is that the longer you live in the world that God created, the more you will know of his incomparably great power through faith in his Son. "That power is like the working of his mighty strength, which he exerted in Christ when he raised him from the dead" (Eph. 1:19).

Before moving on to the next chapter, pause and meditate on the power of God in creation, using the words of the well-known hymn by Isaac Watts, "I Sing the Almighty Power of God":

> I sing th'almighty pow'r of God that made the
>> mountains rise,
> That spread the flowing seas abroad and built the
>> lofty skies.
> I sing the wisdom that ordained the sun to rule
>> the day;
> The moon shines full at his command and all the
>> stars obey.

I sing the goodness of the Lord that filled the
　　earth with food;
He formed the creatures with his word, and then
　　pronounced them good.
Lord, how your wonders are displayed where'er I
　　turn my eye,
If I survey the ground I tread or gaze upon the
　　sky!

There's not a plant or flow'r below but makes
　　your glories known;
And clouds arise and tempests blow by order from
　　your throne;
While all that borrows life from you is ever in your
　　care,
And everywhere that man can be, you, God, are
　　present there.

QUESTIONS FOR PERSONAL REFLECTION
OR GROUP DISCUSSION

1. Where do you see God's power displayed in creation
in the area in which you live?
2. How have you felt in the face of God's power displayed in tornadoes, earthquakes, hurricanes, and
the like?
3. Is prayer for God's power in your life a regular part
of your prayers? Why?
4. Where would you like to see God's power at work in
your life? Do you believe that that power is already at
work within you?

Chapter Three

Witness to the Wisdom of God

How many are your works, O LORD!
    In wisdom you made them all;
       the earth is full of your creatures. (Ps. 104:24)

Give thanks to the LORD, for he is good . . .
to him who alone does great wonders . . .
who by his understanding made the heavens. (Ps. 136:1, 4–5)

"Tell them this: 'These gods, who did not make the heavens and the
earth, will perish from the earth and from under the heavens.'"
But God made the earth by his power;
    he founded the world by his wisdom
      and stretched out the heavens by his understanding.
        (Jer. 10:11–12)

Notice these sentences from the quotations above: "In wisdom you made them all." "By his understanding [God] made the heavens." "He founded the world by his wisdom and stretched out the heavens by his understanding." This theme runs throughout the Scriptures: God used his infinite wisdom to create the world.

Now, because God used his infinite wisdom to create, we are able to see that wisdom reflected in the creation. There is not a single place in the universe that does not testify to the wisdom of God. It pervades the whole universe. The Scriptures teach what our experience confirms: creation bears witness to the wisdom of God.

So, what can we learn from the Bible about the wisdom of God as it is displayed in creation? First, that God has ordained laws to govern his creation. Second, that these laws display his wisdom. And third, that God's wisdom becomes ours as we learn to live in keeping with these laws. Let's take a look at some of the laws that God has ordained for his creation.

GOD'S LAWS GOVERN HIS CREATION

His Laws Govern the Whole Universe

Like Abraham, Isaac, and Jacob, Job was a patriarch. He lived about the same time as the other patriarchs, but he seems to have lived in the area of Haran, where Abraham's relatives lived. At first, Job was wealthy and healthy and had a large family. But then Job experienced tremendous suffering: he lost his wealth, his children, and his health. His pain was aggravated by his confusion concerning what the Lord was doing in his life. In his own time, God responded to Job by asking him a series of questions, including these two: "Do you know the laws of the heavens? Can you set up [God's] dominion over the earth?" (Job 38:33).

Look at those questions again. The first one refers to the heavens, while the second one refers to the earth. This is an Old Testament way of referring to the whole universe.

Go outside on a cloudless afternoon and look up. You will see a big, blue expanse. That expanse, and everything above it, corresponds to "the heavens" in the phrase "the heavens and the earth." "The earth," then, is everything beneath the blue expanse.

The question the Lord raises is, "Do you know the laws, not just of the heavens or the earth, but of the entire universe?" The word "law" is a translation of the Hebrew word *choq* (which sounds something like *coke*). We will encounter the word *choq* (often translated "decree") in many texts in the course of this chapter.

"Job, do you know the decrees of the heavens?" God asked. "Can you set up my dominion over the earth? Do you set up the rules that govern the universe? Job, do you understand all of the laws I have put in place and by which I govern the universe? Do you have the wisdom to govern the universe? Do you want to try it for a day? Do you want to set up the rules that make all the galaxies stay in their positions, and the earth go around the sun, and the moon go around the earth, and the earth rotate on its axis? Do you want to try it?" Job had no answers.

Job did not understand these laws of the universe. He certainly did not control them. God did, and he still does. These laws govern the whole universe—the heavens and the earth.

His Laws Are Specific

When the Bible speaks of the laws of creation, it is not really talking about what some philosophers would call "natural law": laws that by themselves govern the creation. Nor do scientific laws govern the creation. Scientific laws are merely descriptions of the regular means by which a personal God governs the universe he has made. In other words, the laws that govern the creation are not autonomous; they are not laws unto themselves. In reality they are theonomous; that is, they are subject to God. They are the laws by which God personally governs the world he has made.

You see, we do not live in a random, chance universe. We live in a universe that is governed by a personal God, who issues personal commands to the creation, so that it does what he wants it to do.

God's Laws Govern the Sun, the Moon, and the Stars. In the Bible we discover that God has laws, or decrees, that govern the heavenly bodies.

> This is what the LORD says,
> he who appoints the sun
>   to shine by day,
> who decrees the moon and stars
>   to shine by night,
> who stirs up the sea
>   so that its waves roar—
>   the LORD Almighty is his name:
> "Only if these decrees vanish from my sight,"
>   declares the LORD,
> "will the descendants of Israel ever cease
>   to be a nation before me." (Jer. 31:35–36)

God has issued decrees that keep the sun, the moon, and the stars operating day after day, year after year. Why does the earth go around the sun and not stop? Because God has commanded the earth to orbit the sun. So, too, the moon circles the earth and the stars travel in predictable courses. God's decrees govern all the heavenly bodies. But God's laws do more than direct the heavens; they even direct events on earth.

God's Laws Govern the Rain. By his decree, God also governs the rain.

> When he established the force of the wind
>   and measured out the waters,
> when he made a decree for the rain
>   and a path for the thunderstorm,
> then he looked at wisdom and appraised it;
>   he confirmed it and tested it. (Job 28:25–27)

Why does rain fall? On one level, rain falls because the air becomes saturated with water. But why does the air become saturated with water? Because God has issued a command, a decree, that governs the amount of moisture that air can hold at a given temperature. God's law governs the falling of the rain.

God's Laws Govern the Seashore. My family likes to go to the beach. Once, after a full day there, as we were driving away, one of my children asked, "Could a big wave get us now?" He wanted to know how far inland the ocean could come. It can come only as far as God allows, because he has issued a decree and said, "This far, and no farther."

God's laws govern the boundaries between the land and the sea. Proverbs 8:29 refers to a time "when he gave the sea its boundary so the waters would not overstep his command." The word "boundary" translates the Hebrew word *choq*. This word is difficult to translate in this text because it has two senses at the same time. On the one hand, *choq* refers to the seashore, hence the translation "boundary." But the meaning "decree" is also present, as is indicated by the parallel word at the end of the sentence, "command." The full sense is, "God set the decree in place that governs the shoreline by saying to the ocean, 'You are allowed to come this far, but no farther.'"

God's Laws Govern Human Destiny. God's laws even govern human destiny. In Job 14:5, we read,

> Man's days are determined;
>> you have decreed the number of his months
>> and have set limits he cannot exceed.

Human destiny is controlled, not by chance, not by impersonal fate, but by the sovereign command of God. This is why Paul says in Acts 17:26,

> From one man he made every nation of men, that they should inhabit the whole earth; and he determined the times set for them and the exact places where they should live.

We do not live in a random universe, nor do we live in a universe of chance. We live in a universe that is governed by the laws of God. Not just moral laws like "You shall not kill," but also laws of creation like "Earth, you shall go around the sun. . . . Moon, you shall rotate around the earth. . . . Earth, you shall spin at just the right speed, tilted at just the right angle." Everything in the whole universe, from the courses of the stars to the number of hairs on your head, is governed by the command of almighty God.

What the Bible refers to as God's law of creation, using the word *choq,* is an aspect of what is called the providence of God. For example, The Westminster Shorter Catechism (a Reformed question-and-answer summary of the Bible's teaching, completed in 1647) asks in question 11, "What are God's works of providence?" The answer is, "God's works of providence are, his most holy, wise, and powerful preserving and governing all his creatures, and all their actions." In other words, God's providence is his wise care and control of everything he has made, including human destiny.

His Laws Are Unbreakable

Unbreakable by the Creation. God's laws of creation are unbreakable. That is, they are unbreakable by the creation itself.

Humans can't break them.

> Man's days are determined;
> > you have decreed the number of his months
> > and have set limits he *cannot exceed.* (Job 14:5)

Nonhuman creation can't break them.

> [Wisdom was there] when he gave the sea its
> > boundary
> > so the waters would *not overstep* his command.
> > (Prov. 8:29)

> "Should you not fear me?" declares the LORD.
> > "Should you not tremble in my presence?
> I made the sand a boundary for the sea,
> > an everlasting barrier it *cannot cross.*

The waves may roll, but they cannot prevail;
    they may roar, but they *cannot cross* it."
        (Jer. 5:22)

You set a boundary they *cannot cross;*
    never again will they cover the earth.
        (Ps. 104:9)

God's laws governing creation can never be broken.

He set them in place for ever and ever;
    he gave a decree that will *never pass away.*
        (Ps. 148:6)

These texts are particularly interesting because they all combine a Hebrew word for "not" with the verb *avar,* which is translated "exceed," "overstep," "cross," and "pass away." In many other texts, however, *avar* means "transgress." Like *choq* in Proverbs 8:29, "not *avar*" in the texts just quoted is difficult to translate, because two senses are intended at the same time. For example, in Proverbs 8:29, Jeremiah 5:22, and Psalm 104:9, "not *avar*" refers to the sea (1) not crossing the shoreline and (2) not transgressing God's law of creation. Psalm 148:6 refers to the sun, the moon, and the stars (1) not leaving their courses and (2) not transgressing God's law of creation. In one sense, Job 14:5 says that each one of us has a number of days that we cannot exceed; but, on another level, we must understand that this is a matter of God's decree that cannot be transgressed.

But Not Unbreakable by God. These laws may be unbreakable, but not for God. Having earlier introduced the idea of providence, I want to make an important distinction at this point.

There is a difference between God's ordinary providence and his extraordinary providence. When we are talking about the laws of creation by which God governs the universe, we are talking about God's ordinary providence, or his wise governing of his creation. His ordinary providence is the way he usually governs.

But there is also God's extraordinary providence. This is the unusual, extraordinary way in which God works. Miracles are one type of extraordinary providence. God usually works by his ordinary providence, but sometimes he works by his extraordinary providence.

Most of the time I go to bed at 10:00 P.M., but I am not under any obligation to do so. I can go to bed earlier (if my children permit!), or I can stay up until midnight (if I have the energy). So, although I generally do things one way, I am free to do them other ways. Similarly, God ordinarily does things in certain ways, but he is not bound to do them that way all the time. He is free to govern the universe in extraordinary ways from time to time to accomplish his good purpose.

The sun usually tracks across the horizon at a steady pace, but once it stood still (see Josh. 10:12–13). While neither you nor I could cause such a thing to happen, it is no problem for God. He does not have to do things the same way all the time. Since he had the power to create it all, he has the power to govern it any way he wants.

We can observe in the creation how God ordinarily works. But we must not put God in a box and say that he can only work in those ordinary, usual ways. As the Creator, who speaks the command to make the universe operate, God is free to govern his world in extraordinary ways from time to time for his own purposes.

God's laws of creation do more than regulate the operation of the universe; these laws also display his wisdom.

GOD'S LAWS OF CREATION DISPLAY HIS WISDOM

Law and Wisdom

> When he established the force of the wind
> and measured out the waters,
> when he made a decree [*choq*] for the rain
> and a path for the thunderstorm,
> then he looked at wisdom and appraised it;
> he confirmed it and tested it. (Job 28:25–27)

There is an apparent *non sequitur* in this text: the "then" clause doesn't seem to follow the "when" clauses. We would expect the text to say that when God "established the force of the wind and measured out the waters, when he made a decree for the rain and a path for the thunderstorm, then he looked at the *laws of creation* and appraised them." But the text says, "then he looked at *wisdom* and appraised it"! The text replaces "the laws of creation" with "wisdom" because the writer considered the laws of creation to be the same as the wisdom of God.

Wisdom can be compared to the blueprint that a builder uses or to the owner's manual that explains how to put something together and use it as originally intended. God's wisdom is like a blueprint or an owner's manual for governing the universe. Just as an architect's wisdom is displayed in intricate blueprints and then translated by a builder into a beautiful home, so God's wisdom is also seen in his creation.

Creation and Wisdom

Since God's laws display his wisdom, and these laws govern the creation, the creation itself must manifest the wisdom of God. And it does. The creation tells us not only that God is, but that he is wise.

Read the whole of Psalm 104. It's a magnificent poem about God's creating and governing all his creatures and all their actions. Right in the middle of this meditation, the wisdom of God in creation so overwhelms the psalmist that he must exclaim, "How many are your works, O LORD! In wisdom you made them all" (v. 24).

When you look at creation, you see not only the wisdom of God, but also the wisdom of a God whose creative works are wonderful. In Psalm 136 we read,

> Give thanks to the LORD, for he is good . . . :
> to him who alone does great wonders, . . .
> who by his understanding made the heavens.
> (vv. 1, 4, 5)

Now, I may not be a scientist, yet the more closely I examine the creation, the more I am filled with wonder at what God has done in creating the universe.

My wife and I once spent several days in the desert at Palm Springs. One afternoon we took an excursion up the Palm Springs Tram, ascending the San Jacinto Mountains to an elevation of eight thousand feet in fifteen minutes. I walked by myself for about five minutes and found myself in complete solitude, looking out over miles of God-made mountains and valleys. I cannot describe what I was thinking and feeling with any words better than those of the psalmist:

> Give thanks to the LORD, for he is good . . . :
> to him who alone does *great wonders*, . . .
> who by his understanding made the heavens.

When you consider the magnificence of the universe, you too can be full of wonder at the wonderful Creator who made it and governs it all.

Creation also displays the wisdom of the true and living God. God said to Jeremiah,

> Tell them this: "These gods, who did not make the heavens and the earth, will perish from the earth and from under the heavens." But God made the earth by his power; he founded the world by his wisdom and stretched out the heavens by his understanding. (Jer. 10:11–12)

In Jeremiah's day, there were many false gods who were identified with various aspects of creation—for example, Aten, the Egyptian god of the sun, or Baal, the Canaanite god of the storm, or Ishtar, the Babylonian goddess associated with Venus, the morning star. In such a culture, Jeremiah had to affirm the biblical truth that the true and living God cannot be identified with any aspect of the creation. Worshiping creation is not the same as worshiping God. The true and living God is different; he is set apart from the entire creation. He is not identical with the sun or the moon or the stars. Rather, he is the one who by his great wisdom created the sun, the moon, and the stars—and all of heaven and earth.

In our own day, we see a reemergence of worshiping the creation. A goddess is identified with this or that part of the creation, and with the earth in particular. Some call her Mother Earth. Others call her Gaia. As Christians, we must affirm what Jeremiah affirmed: there is a distinction between the creation and the Creator. When we look at the creation, we are driven to worship, but we must not worship the creation. It merely displays the beautiful wisdom of the true and living God, who alone is to be worshiped.

How does creation display God's wisdom? Let's look at several examples of God's wisdom in creation, as it is displayed on our own planet.

God's Wisdom and Earth's Gravity. If earth's gravitational pull were any greater than it is, ammonia and methane could not escape the gravitation pull of the earth, and life would be impossible, because we could not live with high levels of these gases in our atmosphere. If earth's gravitational pull were significantly less than it is, water vapor would escape too rapidly, and life would be impossible, because the water cycle necessary for life could not operate. A little more gravity, or a little less, and there would be no life.

God's Wisdom and Earth's Distance. If the earth were a little farther from the sun, our planet would be too cold, and life would be impossible. However, if the earth were a little closer to the sun, it would be too hot, and life would be impossible.

God's Wisdom and Earth's Rotation. If the earth's rotation were slower, the difference in temperature between day and night would be too great, and life would be impossible. If the earth's rotation were faster, wind velocity would be too great, and life would be impossible.

God's Wisdom and Earth's Moon. If the moon's gravitational pull were just a little greater or a little less, the water cycle (precipitation, run off, evaporation) would not be possible, and life would be impossible.

God's Wisdom and Earth's People. Think of a newborn baby. Nine months earlier, that baby did not exist. Then one sperm and one egg met, nine months passed, and a human being was born with intelligence, vision, speech, hearing, and movement. Wonderful! The wisdom of God!

All of creation testifies to God's wisdom, from cosmic black holes to DNA strands. If God has the wisdom to govern the whole universe, doesn't he also have the wisdom to govern your life? Will you trust him to do that? Think about the universe and then ask yourself, Who could govern the universe better than he? If God can govern the entire universe, how much more can he govern your life down to the smallest details?

The testimony to the wisdom of God that is found in the world of God is also found in the Word of God.

> For you created my inmost being;
>> you knit me together in my mother's womb.
> I praise you because I am fearfully and wonder-
>>> fully made;
>> your works are wonderful,
>> I know that full well.
> My frame was not hidden from you
>> when I was made in the secret place.
> When I was woven together in the depths of the
>>> earth,
>> your eyes saw my unformed body.
> All the days ordained for me
>> were written in your book
>> before one of them came to be.
> How precious to me are your thoughts, O God!
>> How vast is the sum of them! (Ps. 139:13–17)

Just contemplating the wisdom of God displayed in the universe can create within us a tranquil, childlike trust.

> Trust in the LORD with all your heart
>> and lean not on your own understanding;
> in all of your ways acknowledge him,
>> and he will make your paths straight.
>>> (Prov. 3:5–6)

Our God is infinitely wise. We must admit that we do not always understand his wisdom, because his thoughts are not our thoughts and his ways are not our ways.

> As the heavens are higher than the earth,
>   so are my ways higher than your ways
>   and my thoughts than your thoughts.
>   (Isa. 55:9)

Yet, even when we do not understand, we can be confident that he governs his creatures and their actions with infinite wisdom.

GOD'S LAWS REQUIRE US TO STUDY AND CONFORM

Since God is all-wise in governing his creation, including our lives, we must learn to live in accordance with God's wise laws displayed in creation. How do we do that? Let me suggest three ways.

By Observing Creation

The Bible tells us to observe creation in order to learn how to live.

> I went past the field of the sluggard,
>   past the vineyard of the man who lacks judg-
>   ment;
> thorns had come up everywhere,
>   the ground was covered with weeds,
>   and the stone wall was in ruins.
> I applied my heart to what I observed
>   and learned a lesson from what I saw:

"A little sleep, a little slumber,
    a little folding of the hands to rest—
and poverty will come on you like a bandit
    and scarcity like an armed man."
                (Prov. 24:30–34)

The Ancient Wise Man. The ancient wise man observed the world, thought about his observations, formed a conclusion, and then put that conclusion into a proverb. He observed a lazy man's field, with its thorns and weeds and broken-down wall. He thought, "I wonder if there is a connection between the laziness of the man and the state of the field?" He concluded, "If you are lazy, then your field is going to be in disrepair." He composed a proverb to capture this insight into the way God's world works, so that others might benefit. This is a good way to see the wisdom of God in the world.

The Modern Wise Man. The scientist certainly is "wise" in a special way, because what we read about in Proverbs 24 is analogous to basic scientific methodology. Scientists have a wonderful calling to observe the universe that God has made, to think about those observations, to form a conclusion, and to communicate that conclusion so that others may benefit from it.

For example, suppose a scientist stands on a balcony seven floors up, takes a bunch of baseballs, and then drops them one at a time. He observes that they all go down. He concludes that there must be a force at work pulling the baseballs down. He thinks, "I'll call this *gravity*. And if I wish to continue living, I'd better pay attention and not step off the balcony, because, unless God does something extraordinary, I'll not go up or right or left, but down."

All of us can be engaged in this wisdom-gathering process. On an unsophisticated level, this is what some might call sanctified common sense. All of us need to be observing the world in which we live, thinking about our observations, and forming useful conclusions.

Observe the world. You'll notice patterns emerging. The universe is not random, but is ordered by God, who controls it by his great wisdom.

Now, this observation of the world is not a neutral observation. It is not an autonomous observation, made as if we were on our own and God were not involved. We are actually listening for God's voice when we observe his creation. So, we learn to live in accordance with God's wisdom, not only by observing God's world, but also by listening to God.

By Listening to God

The book of Isaiah contains an exquisite poem about a wise farmer:

> Listen and hear my voice;
>   pay attention and hear what I say.
> When a farmer plows for planting, does he plow
>   continually?
>   Does he keep on breaking up and harrowing
>   the soil?
> When he has leveled the surface,
>   does he not sow caraway and scatter cummin?
> Does he not plant wheat in its place,
>   barley in its plot,
>   and spelt in its field?
> *His God instructs him*
>   *and teaches him the right way.*
> Caraway is not threshed with a sledge,
>   nor is a cartwheel rolled over cummin;
> caraway is beaten out with a rod,
>   and cummin with a stick.

Grain must be ground to make bread;
   so one does not go on threshing it forever.
Though he drives the wheels of his threshing cart
      over it,
   his horses do not grind it.
All this also comes from the LORD Almighty,
   wonderful in counsel and magnificent in wisdom.
     (Isa. 28:23–29)

Do you know any farmers who plow twelve months out of the year and never sow seed? At the end of those twelve months, do any say, "Well, I think I'm going to spend the next twelve months plowing some more"? No farmer does that. After plowing, the farmer plants, just as God said to Isaiah. The farmer also knows that some ways of processing grain are better for one kind of grain and that other ways are better for another kind. How did the farmer learn all this? By luck? No way! Isaiah says, "His God instructs him and teaches him the right way. . . . All this also comes from the LORD Almighty, wonderful in counsel and magnificent in wisdom."

Now, you'll look in vain in the Bible to find any directions on how to plow or on which kind of processing to use for specific grains. God instructed the farmer, but not by means of the Bible. God instructed the farmer by the way of wisdom, as he observed creation. By observing the seasons and experimenting with various plants, the farmer learned when to plow, when to plant, and when to harvest his crops. As he did, God was there instructing him. God instructs us by giving us wisdom to live in the world.

There is an interface, an interplay, between God's instruction in the Bible and his instruction in creation. We need both. We must listen to the voice of God in creation, because there are things we can learn there for practical living that are not taught in the Bible. It is all God's law, whether it is in the creation or in the Bible. We must know God's law in order to live in this world. When we learn God's law in creation and in the Bible, and when we live in accordance with that law, the Bible says that we are displaying wisdom. Wisdom is not just knowing the law of God, but also living in accordance with it.

While listening to God in his world and listening to him in his Word are complementary, his revelation in his Word has priority over his revelation in his world. Among other reasons, there is a greater precision of revelation in the propositions of the Bible than in the sparrow's nesting habits. We read the book of nature through the lens of the book of Scripture. The Scriptures alone teach us to live in accordance with God's wisdom by trusting in Christ.

By Trusting Christ

Of course, we must live in accordance with God's law by trusting in Christ. Paul says in Colossians 2:3 that Christ is the one "in whom are hidden all the treasures of wisdom and knowledge." When Paul uses the word "wisdom," he has the Old Testament concept of wisdom in mind. Complete wisdom is found in Christ.

In 1 Corinthians 1:30, Paul says, "You are in Christ Jesus, who has become for us wisdom from God—that is, our righteousness, holiness and redemption." When Paul defines *wisdom*, the first word he uses is *righteousness*. In the Old Testament, *righteousness* fundamentally means "right order, conformity." Righteousness is conformity to God's will, whether that is conformity to God's will in the Bible or to his will in creation.

We have all failed to be righteous, however. We have failed to be wise. Has anyone lived in perfect conformity to God's will in the Bible? Has anyone lived in perfect conformity to God's will in creation? We all lack wisdom; we are foolish by nature, not wise.

Each problem we have with the environment is a testimony against us that we are not living in conformity to God's Word or his world. If we were, we would not have environmental problems. We need a wisdom that is outside of us, because the result of our foolishness is death.

That is why Paul says that Christ has become our wisdom, that is, our righteousness. Christ has perfectly conformed to the will of God in our place—both the will of God in creation and his will in the Bible. When we trust Christ, God clothes us with Jesus' perfectly wise and righteous life. God looks at us as perfectly wise, although we still act rather unwisely much of the time.

Moreover, 1 Corinthians emphasizes the cross as the manifestation of both God's power and his wisdom. Do you want to see the wisdom of God? Look at the cross, because there you will see death. Death is the result of our foolish rebellion against God's law. But this one death reverses our folly and its consequences. This one death ensures that God's wise plan will ultimately be worked out, not only in the lives of those who trust in Christ, but also in the entire universe he has made.

Considering the wisdom of God in creation forces us, as everything forces us, to renew our trust in Christ. He is the wisdom we need, not only so that the Father can view us as wise, even though we are not, but also so that we might know how to live with wisdom in the world God has made.

In Christ are all of the treasures of God's wisdom. When we trust Christ, we can look into the Word and into the world, discerning the wisdom of God and laying hold of the power to live in accordance with that wisdom.

May God grant us grace to see his wisdom, to live in conformity to that wisdom, and to experience what the Bible calls abundant life. A hymn that pulls these themes together in a marvelous way is Edmund Clowney's "Vast the Immensity":

Vast the immensity, mirror of majesty,
Galaxies spread in a curtain of light:
Lord, your eternity rises in mystery
There where no eye can see, infinite height!

Sounds your creative word, forming both star and
        bird,
Shaping the cosmos to win your delight;
Order from chaos springs, form that your wisdom
        brings,
Guiding created things, infinite might!

Who can your wisdom scan? Who comprehend
        your plan?
How can the mind of man your truth embrace?
Here does your Word disclose more than your
        power shows,
Love that to Calv'ry goes, infinite grace!

Triune your majesty, triune your love to me,
Fixed from eternity in heav'n above.
Father, what mystery, in your infinity
You gave your Son for me, infinite love!

QUESTIONS FOR PERSONAL REFLECTION OR GROUP DISCUSSION

1. In what ways do you see God's wisdom in creation?
2. How are God's speaking through the Bible and through the creation related?
3. In what areas of your life can you gain wisdom by listening to God speak through his creation?
4. What can you do to learn more about nature?

Chapter Four

Witness to the
Love of God

O LORD, you preserve both man and beast.
How priceless is your unfailing love! (Ps. 36:6b–7a)

The LORD is faithful to all his promises
and loving toward all he has made. (Ps. 145:13b)

In Lystra there sat a man crippled in his feet, who was lame from birth
and had never walked. He listened to Paul as he was speaking. Paul
looked directly at him, saw that he had faith to be healed and called out,
"Stand up on your feet!" At that, the man jumped up and began to walk.

When the crowd saw what Paul had done, they shouted in the Ly-
caonian language, "The gods have come down to us in human form!"
Barnabas they called Zeus, and Paul they called Hermes because he
was the chief speaker. The priest of Zeus, whose temple was just outside the city, brought bulls and wreaths to the city gates because he and
the crowd wanted to offer sacrifices to them.

But when the apostles Barnabas and Paul heard of this, they tore
their clothes and rushed out into the crowd, shouting: "Men, why are

*you doing this? We too are only men, human like you. We are bringing
you good news, telling you to turn from these worthless things to the
living God, who made heaven and earth and sea and everything in them.
In the past, he let all nations go their own way. Yet he has not left himself without testimony: He has shown kindness by giving you rain from
heaven and crops in their seasons; he provides you with plenty of food
and fills your hearts with joy." (Acts 14:8–17)*

The word translated "unfailing love" in Psalm 36 is the
word typically used in the Old Testament for God's covenantal love, by which he saves his people from their sins. This is
quite an amazing text because the psalmist is saying that
when he looks at God's preservation—not just the salvation
of his people, but his preservation of the whole created order, people, and animals—he sees God's covenantal love.
He sees this preservation and exclaims that God's love is
priceless. Perhaps we are too accustomed to thinking of
God's love only in terms of his relationship with his children. Perhaps we are too accustomed to viewing creation
only as a resource to meet our needs. This amazing text de-
clares creation to be the object of God's unfailing love!

Yes, there is a general love that God has for the whole of
his creation. God doesn't simply care for his creation out of
a sense of duty to sustain what he has created. Rather, the
Bible portrays God as caring for his creation because he
loves it. He loves it with a priceless, unfailing love.

Paul's audience in the Acts 14 passage is in many ways
like an audience in the United States today. The people of
Lystra are so confused theologically that when they see
God's care displayed in the healing of a crippled man, they
mistakenly think that Paul and Barnabas must be gods! But
Paul and Barnabas quickly point out that they are human
beings, not gods (v. 15), and they turn their audience's attention away from the false ideas that fill their minds to the

truth of the living God. They identify the true and living God as the Creator of heaven and earth and the seas and everything in them (v. 15).

Paul says to these people, who don't know the Bible, "Yet [God] has not left himself without testimony" (v. 17). In creation there is a testimony to God's kindness, his love. Having witnessed the healing of the crippled man, these people have sufficient evidence to conclude that there is a true and living God who loves his creation.

Something as simple as the rain tells us not just that God is there, but that the God who is there is a God who loves and cares for the creation he has made (Acts 14:17).

This idea that God loves his creation was not original to Paul. It is also found in the Old Testament.

GOD'S LOVE FOR CREATION IS SEEN AT THE TIME OF CREATION

We use the word *creation* in two ways: for God's *act* of creating and for the *result* of that act. A synonym for the second meaning, creation as result, is the word *nature*. But at this point I want to look at the first meaning: creation in the sense of God's *act* of creating.

God's Love Is Seen in the Order That He Established at Creation

Genesis 1:1 tells of God creating the universe, the heavens and the earth, the visible and invisible realms (see Col. 1:16). Verse 2 then describes the earth as formless and empty. Not everything was in order. Although God had created matter and energy, and everything necessary for life was there, it wasn't in the right order for there to be life. At that initial stage, life was impossible. The text goes on to describe how God brought about order in six orderly days. The creation account emphasizes order to teach us that there is great order in creation. God created a place for everything, and he put everything in its place.

The Genesis record divides the story of creation into two three-day periods. The focus of the first three days is on God's creating a place for everything. On Day 1, God brought order by separating the light from the darkness. On Day 2, he brought order by separating the space above the sky from the space below the sky. On Day 3, he brought order by separating the dry land from the seas. God created all the distinct compartments, we might say, in the universe.

The focus of the second three-day period is on God's putting everything in its place. On Day 4, he filled the heavens with luminaries: sun, moon, and stars. On Day 5, he filled the seas with fish and the skies with birds. And on Day 6, God filled the earth with animals and created human beings as the apex of his work.

By the end of God's creative work, the earth, the sea, and the sky were teeming with life. He did not simply make life possible; he made abundant life possible. God loved his creation enough to establish order in it, so that abundant life would be possible.

God's Love Is Seen in His Making Everything Good

"And God saw that it was good." Genesis 1 repeats this phrase six times before the climactic statement, "God saw all that he had made, and it was very good" (v. 31). What does "good" mean?

In Genesis 1, "good" means "just right for the intended purpose." Let me explain. A baseball bat is good for hitting a ball. But would a bat be good for getting a splinter out of your finger? Of course not. "Good" in Genesis 1 means "good for the intended purpose."

God saw that the light was good (v. 3), just right for its intended purpose. The purpose of light is to provide an environment for life, for without light there isn't any life. That is why the Bible often joins the themes of light and life. The psalmist says, "With you is the fountain of *life;* in your *light* we see light" (Ps. 36:9). Jesus said, "I am the *light* of the world. Whoever follows me will never walk in darkness, but will have *the light of life*" (John 8:12). Light and life are joined together in the Word of God, because they are joined together in the world of God. Without light there is no life. The light was good, good for the purpose of fostering life.

God saw that the separation of the land from the sea was good (Gen. 1:10): just right for fish and aquatic life, and just right for plant, animal, and human life. The separation of the dry land from the sea was good, because it was just right for God's intended purpose. God saw that the vegetation was good (v. 12), just right for human consumption (v. 29) and for animal fodder (v. 30). The vegetation was good, just right for God's intended purpose.

God saw that the sun, the moon, and the stars were good (v. 18), just right for dividing time—for marking seasons, days, months, and years—just right for providing light for the day and light for the night. Have you ever noticed that night is not pitch black? What would night be like if it were? God has ordered the world so that there is just enough light for the night.

God saw that the fish and the birds were good (v. 21), just right for swimming in the seas and flying in the air. Some fish jump out of the water and give the appearance of flying, but they always land back in the water. Some birds dive under water, but they always come back up, because it's not "good" or "just right" for birds to live in the sea or for fish to live in the air. God made everything just right for his intended purpose.

God saw that the land animals were good (v. 25), just right for living on the land. Then the climax of this passage comes: "God saw all that he had made, and it was *very good*" (v. 31). Everything was just right for his intended purpose.

Notice that seven "goods" run through the account, and, of course, seven is often a symbol for perfection. So, when the Bible says that the creation was good, good, good, good, good, good, and very good, it's saying that the creation was perfect.

In fact, there are numerous plays on the number seven in Genesis 1:1–2:3. Consider just a few: (1) "God" occurs thirty-five (7x5) times; (2) "earth" occurs twenty-one (7x3) times; (3) the introduction (vv. 1–2) has twenty-one (7x3) words in Hebrew: verse 1 has seven words, and verse 2 has fourteen (7x2) words; and (4) the conclusion (2:1–3) has thirty-five (7x5) words. The number seven, perfection, is woven into the fabric of the text. God was careful, full of care, to make a creation that was utterly perfect. As someone once said, "God doesn't make junk." He loved enough to make a perfect creation.

God's Love Is Seen in His Making a Caretaker for Everything

God created humans, male and female together, to rule over the creation that he had made (Gen. 1:26–29). This rulership includes taking care of the creation.

God loved his creation, and so he placed Adam in the garden to work it and to take care of it (2:15). Sometimes God manifests his love for his creation directly, but often he manifests his love indirectly through our care for it. While there are extreme positions on the issue of environmentalism, the Bible teaches a balanced view of our responsibility to care for the creation and our right to use it to meet human needs. My purpose here is simply to point out that God's making a caretaker for creation is evidence of his love for the creation.

God has not left himself without a witness, and in many ways the creation account in Genesis teaches us that the creation testifies that God is full of love for his creation.

GOD'S LOVE FOR CREATION IS SEEN AT THE TIME OF THE FLOOD

It may seem odd to say that God's love for creation is seen at the time of the Flood. Didn't God say in Genesis 6:7, "I will wipe mankind, whom I have created, from the face of the earth—men and animals, and creatures that move along the ground, and birds of the air—for I am grieved that I have made them"? How can God show his love when he destroys his creation? It may seem hard to believe, but God left a testimony of his love in the Flood.

God Loved Noah and His Family

God determined to destroy the human race, but not entirely. He loved Noah and his family. God decided to preserve one man and his family, not because they were more righteous than others, but because God gave them his undeserved favor: "But Noah found favor in the eyes of the LORD" (Gen. 6:8). God loved Noah and his family so much that he taught them how to be saved from the coming flood by building an ark.

God Cared for the Animals

God also loved the animals, which could not have survived the Flood. He did not show his love to them directly, but indirectly through Noah.

> You are to bring into the ark two of all living crea-
> tures, male and female, *to keep them alive* with you.
> Two of every kind of bird, of every kind of animal
> and of every kind of creature that moves along the
> ground will come to you *to be kept alive.* You are to
> take every kind of food that is to be eaten and store
> it away as food for you *and for them."* (Gen. 6:19–21)

Even while he was destroying the rest of the living creatures, God demonstrated his love for the creation by requir-
ing Noah to keep pairs of animals alive. He required the
preservation of a male and a female of each kind so that the
animals would be able to reproduce after the Flood. God intended to fill the earth with life once again.

God had enough love to instruct Noah to bring sufficient food for the animals, just as God had provided food at
the time of creation. Even during the Flood, God had
enough love to preserve human and nonhuman life.

God Loved the Whole Creation

God didn't simply love people and animals; he also
loved the whole creation. This love is seen in the beautiful
little poem in Genesis 8:22:

As long as the earth endures,

will never cease.

The order of the words "seedtime and harvest, cold and
heat, summer and winter, day and night" may seem to be

random. In fact, the order forms an intricate pattern of two overlaid *X*s. In Israel, seedtime is in winter, just after the fall rains have ended five months of drought. Harvest is in summer, just after the spring rains have brought the grain to maturity. Cold is at night and heat is during the day. The point is that after the Flood, God loved his creation enough to maintain its beautiful order.

Not only can we say that God doesn't make any junk, but we can also say that God doesn't junk what he's made. He created for his glory. And even though he brought judgment on the earth, he didn't junk it. He was concerned to preserve his creation through the divine judgment.

GOD'S LOVE FOR CREATION IS SEEN AT THE PRESENT TIME

Not just at the time of creation, not just at the Flood, but even today, God's love is seen as he sustains his creation and provides for it. Let's take a look at these concepts.

God Shows His Love by Sustaining All He Has Made

"The Son is the radiance of God's glory and the exact representation of his being, *sustaining all things by his powerful word*" (Heb. 1:3). "He is before all things, and *in him all things hold together*" (Col. 1:17).

Why does the sun shine, day after day? Why does the earth orbit the sun, day after day? Why does the earth rotate at just the right speed, day after day? Why does our moon continue to circle the earth without fail? Why is your heart beating right now, even though you are making no conscious effort to make it beat? Why are your lungs taking in oxygen and expelling carbon dioxide, even though you are not thinking about it? There are scientific answers to all of these questions. But why is it that the scientist has been able to discover these regularities? Because God is love. He loves his creation enough to sustain it, to maintain it, and to uphold it by his powerful word.

The word that was powerful enough to bring the creation into existence is still operating, moment by moment, to maintain it. God sustains his creation by his powerful word as an expression of his love.

God Shows His Love by Providing for All He Has Made

God Provides Sunshine and Rain. Jesus said, "Love your enemies" (Matt 5:44). If you love your enemies, you will show "that you [are] sons of your Father in heaven" (v. 45). Next, Jesus said that the Father "causes his sun to rise on the evil and the good, and sends rain on the righteous and the unrighteous" (v. 45). God's provision of sunshine and rain for both the righteous and the unrighteous is a demonstration of his love for his creation.

Psalm 147:8–9 says,

> He covers the sky with clouds;
> he supplies the earth with rain
> and makes grass grow on the hills.
> He provides food for the cattle
> and for the young ravens when they call.

Why does it rain? In southern California, the hills are quite brown in the fall, since there has been no rain for five months. But in December, after the winter rains have fallen, the hills are covered with greenery—wild grass and shrubs. Why does the wild grass grow in response to the rain? There are valid scientific explanations, but the basis of those explanations is the fundamental truth that God is there. He is there, loving the creation he has made. Therefore, the psalmist gives thanks to God,

> who made the great lights—
>> *His love endures forever.*
> the sun to govern the day,
>> *His love endures forever.*
> the moon and stars to govern the night;
>> *His love endures forever.* (Ps. 136:7–9)

The sun, the moon, and the stars shine as tokens of the Creator's enduring love for his creation.

God Provides Food.

> He waters the mountains from his upper chambers;
>> the earth is satisfied by the fruit of his work.
> He makes grass grow for the cattle,
>> and plants for man to cultivate—
> bringing forth food from the earth:
> wine that gladdens the heart of man,
>> oil to make his face shine,
>> and bread that sustains his heart.
>> (Ps. 104:13–15)

> Give thanks to the LORD, for he is good.
>> *His love endures forever.*
> . . . to him who alone does great wonders,
>> *His love endures forever.*
> . . . and who gives food to every creature.
>> *His love endures forever.* (Ps. 136:1, 4, 25)

The eyes of all look to you,
and you give them their food at the proper
time.
You open your hand
and satisfy the desires of every living thing.
The LORD is righteous in all his ways
and loving toward all he has made.
(Ps. 145:15–17)

Look at the birds of the air; they do not sow or reap
or store away in barns, and yet your heavenly Father
feeds them. (Matt. 6:26)

Birds eat worms because they are fast enough to catch them, have beaks to grasp them, and are able to swallow and digest them. But the Bible provides another perspective, one that complements a scientific perspective. The Bible says that birds eat worms because that's what God feeds them: birds fly to God, he holds out his hand, and birds feed right out of the hand of God. Using this kind of imagery, the Bible teaches us that we do not live in a mechanistic and impersonal universe; rather, we live in a world that is directly and immediately loved by a personal God.

You see, the God of the Bible is not like a watchmaker who winds up a watch and then leaves it to run on its own. The God of the Bible is a personal God who is personally involved, moment by moment, lovingly caring and providing for the creation that he has made.

God Provides Life.

Blessed be your glorious name, and may it be exalted above all blessing and praise. You alone are the LORD. You made the heavens, even the highest heavens, and all their starry host, the earth and all that is on it, the seas and all that is in them. You give life to everything, and the multitudes of heaven worship you. (Neh. 9:5–6)

God gives life, not only to some things, but to everything. Without God there is no life. He loves, and so there is life.

The apostle Paul reminded the Athenians that "in [God] we live and move and have our being" (Acts 17:28). This is true of human beings and of every other life form that God has made. We live and move and have our being in relationship to the God who loves. For if he quit loving for a split second, there would be no life. There is life only because God continues to love.

Moment by moment, creation testifies to the magnificent, priceless love of God.

GOD'S LOVE IS SEEN IN THE NEW CREATION

It is one thing to take care of a car that works right; it's another thing to take care of one that doesn't. It's easy to take care of a healthy child; taking care of a sick child is another story. Similarly, it was one thing for God to take care of his creation before the Fall; it's been another thing for him to take care of it after the Fall, because since then the creation has been groaning. Life is not experienced throughout the created realm in the way that God originally intended.

God Loves This Groaning Creation

In response to Adam's sin, God said to him, "Cursed is the ground because of you" (Gen. 3:17). "In Adam's fall, we sinned all." Our sin as a race (*Adam* means "a man" and "humanity") has brought God's curse on the creation. The created order no longer functions perfectly, as it did before the Fall. Paul picks up this theme in Romans 8, where he says, "The whole creation has been groaning as in the pains of childbirth right up to the present time" (v. 22). Because of our sin, creation is not all that it should be. Creation is groaning under the curse of God, as a woman in labor groans under the curse of God (see Gen. 3:16). The barren womb, miscarriage, and on and on, are not part of God's originally "very good" creation. Yet, God still loves this creation, groaning though it is, and provides for it.

> He covers the sky with clouds;
>> he supplies the earth with rain
>> and makes grass grow on the hills.
> He provides food for the cattle
>> and for the young ravens when they call.
>> (Ps. 147:8–9)

God Loves So Much That He Sent His Son to Redeem This Groaning Creation

When we think of Christ as Redeemer, we think first of him as the Redeemer of God's people. Christ is the Redeemer of those whom the Father gave him before the foundation of the world, those who come to him by faith alone. Christ is the one who delivers people from their sin, not only from the guilt and the power of their sin, but also from the misery of their sin.

Christ the Redeemer is also Christ the Creator. Not only does the Father redeem through the agency of his Son, but he also created through the agency of his Son (John 1:2; Col. 1:16; Heb. 1:10). Christ the Redeemer is not only the Redeemer of fallen human beings, but also the Redeemer of the cursed creation. He has come to save us from our sins and to deliver the whole creation from its groaning.

However, human creation and nonhuman creation are not the objects of redemption in precisely the same way. The nonhuman creation is cursed as a result of our sin, not its own; it has no guilt from which to be delivered. Humans, on the other hand, have sinned against God, have become guilty, and have earned his wrath. But just as our sin resulted in creation being cursed, so our redemption will result in creation being liberated from this curse.

This Redemption Has Already Been Accomplished. In Colossians 1:15–20, Paul teaches us that this redemption has already been accomplished. He says that by Christ "all things were created: things in heaven and on earth, visible and invisible" (v. 16), that "God was pleased to have all his fullness dwell in him" (v. 19), and that through Christ he has reconciled "to himself all things, whether things on earth or things in heaven, by making peace through his blood, shed on the cross" (v. 20).

This reconciliation of all things is first and foremost the reconciliation of rebellious people. Christ comes to redeem us first. But this reconciliation of all things is not just a reconciliation of people, but also the reconciliation of all things. As Paul says in Romans 8, the creation was subjected to frustration, but it was subjected *in hope* (v. 20). The creation has been hoping for liberation from its bondage to decay (v. 21), longing to be freed from the curse. The creation is groaning, but it is also hoping that the blood of Christ, shed on the cross, will bring about its liberation from the bondage and the groaning that it is experiencing. Everything necessary, not only for human salvation, but also for the reconciliation of all things (including the creation) to the Father, has been accomplished through the blood of Christ, shed on the cross.

This Redemption Will Be Fully Experienced at the Second Coming of Christ. In Romans 8, when Paul says that the creation is groaning (v. 22), he also says that we humans are groaning (v. 23). The creation is hoping (v. 20), and so are we (vv. 24–25). We are hoping for "our adoption as sons, the redemption of our bodies" (v. 23): to experience, at our resurrection, the fullness of what it means to be the children of God the Father because we are united to Jesus Christ as our elder brother. Our ultimate hope is not for anything in this life; our hope is in our resurrection from the dead.

The ultimate hope of all creation is for the day of resurrection, because on that day the words of Isaiah will be realized perfectly.

> "Behold, I will create
>   new heavens and a new earth.
> The former things will not be remembered,
>   nor will they come to mind.
> But be glad and rejoice forever
>   in what I will create. . . .
> The wolf and the lamb will feed together,
>   and the lion will eat straw like the ox,
>   but dust will be the serpent's food.
> They will neither harm nor destroy
>   on all my holy mountain,"
>   says the LORD. (Isa. 65:17–18, 25)

On the day of resurrection, the vision of the apostle John will be perfectly realized.

> Then I saw a new heaven and a new earth, for the first heaven and the first earth had passed away, and there was no longer any sea. I saw the Holy City, the new Jerusalem, coming down out of heaven from

God, prepared as a bride beautifully dressed for her husband. And I heard a loud voice from the throne saying, "Now the dwelling of God is with men, and he will live with them. They will be his people, and God himself will be with them and be their God. He will wipe every tear from their eyes. There will be no more death or mourning or crying or pain, for the old order of things has passed away."

He who was seated on the throne said, "I am making everything new!" Then he said, "Write this down, for these words are trustworthy and true." (Rev. 21:1–5)

Just as surely as God preserved the creation through the judgment in the days of Noah, so most assuredly does he promise to preserve this creation through the final judgment. He is going to perfect it and purify it through fire. Creation testifies to the love of God.

HOW CAN WE THEN LIVE?

By Depending on God's Love

Our food doesn't ultimately come from the grocery store, nor our paycheck from our employer. They ultimately come from a God who loves us. We need to develop, day by day, a conscious dependence on the God who is there and who is loving us.

One way we manifest this conscious dependence is through prayer. Jesus said, "This, then, is how you should pray: . . . Give us today our daily bread" (Matt. 6:9, 11). Knowing that food does not come to us automatically, we can acknowledge that it comes to us through the personal care of a personal God, whom we are asking today to give us what we need. Through prayer, we appreciate our life, our breath, our food, our clothing, and our shelter, as we thank God, because we know that in him we live and move and have our being.

By Hoping for God's Love at the Second Coming of Christ

There will be no ecological utopia this side of the resurrection. This truth does not undermine our hope for a better world now; it simply orients our ultimate hope to the same place where the Bible orients it: the coming of Christ, the resurrection from the dead, and the new heavens and the new earth. Similarly, the truth that we will not reach moral perfection in this life, but only in the life to come, does not undermine our present striving to be pure, as Christ is pure (1 John 1:8; 3:2–3). Rather, it fosters it.

By Participating in God's Love

The Bible says that God is going to bring a judgment of fire, just as he brought a judgment of water. But remember, God preserved his creation through the water, and he is going to preserve it through the fire. And just as he loved before the Flood, at the Flood, and after the Flood, so we have the privilege of loving before the fire, at the fire, and after the fire.

Because God has created us in his image (to be like him), and because he loves his creation with a deep love, so we too must love with a deep love. We lovingly preserve the creation, among other reasons, to preserve the witness in creation to the love of God.

By Worshiping the God Who Loves

Nehemiah says,

> Blessed be your glorious name, and may it be exalted above all blessing and praise. You alone are the

LORD. You made the heavens, even the highest heavens, and all their starry host, the earth and all that is on it, the seas and all that is in them. You give life to everything, *and the multitudes of heaven worship you.* (Neh. 9:5–6)

If the multitudes of heaven worship the Creator who cares so much, so can we. We worship God publicly each Sunday and every day of our lives, presenting ourselves to him as living sacrifices, which is our only reasonable response to the great love that he has shown to us in Christ (Rom. 12:1).

Worship him now with the words of the classic hymn, "This Is My Father's World":

> This is my Father's world, and to my list'ning ears,
> All nature sings, and round me rings the music of
>   the spheres.
> This is my Father's world: I rest me in the thought
> Of rocks and trees, of skies and seas; his hand the
>   wonders wrought.
>
> This is my Father's world, the birds their carols
>   raise,
> The morning light, the lily white, declare their
>   Maker's praise.
> This is my Father's world: he shines in all that's
>   fair;
> In the rustling grass I hear him pass, he speaks to
>   me everywhere.
>
> This is my Father's world, O let me ne'er forget
> That though the wrong seems oft so strong, God is
>   the Ruler yet.

This is my Father's world: the battle is not done:
Jesus who died shall be satisfied, and earth and
heav'n be one.

QUESTIONS FOR PERSONAL REFLECTION OR GROUP DISCUSSION

1. How is God's love for creation evident to you?
2. How is God's love for you evident in creation?
3. Do you share God's love for creation? What can you do to see your love for creation grow?
4. What actions can you take to put your love for God's creation into practice in your routine living?

Chapter Five

Witness to the Justice of God

The wrath of God is being revealed from heaven against all the godlessness and wickedness of men who suppress the truth by their wickedness. (Rom. 1:18)

For the creation was subjected to frustration, not by its own choice, but by the will of the one who subjected it, in hope that the creation itself will be liberated from its bondage to decay and brought into the glorious freedom of the children of God. We know that the whole creation has been groaning as in the pains of childbirth right up to the present time. (Rom. 8:20–22)

"The condemnation of the human race is imprinted on the heavens, the earth, and all creatures." Words like these have undoubtedly been proclaimed during celebrations of Earth Day by people concerned about the environment, decrying the pollution and environmental degradation that is evident all around us. This degradation stands as a testimony against the human race.

"The condemnation of the human race is imprinted on

the heavens, the earth, and all creatures." These words, however, are actually John Calvin's. Coming from Calvin's pen, they mean something quite different than if they had been spoken by an environmentalist at an Earth Day celebration.

Suppose that during a celebration of Earth Day, an award were given for the major defiler of the earth. For whom would you vote to win the award? Oil companies? The logging industry? Those who destroy the rain forests? What about people who build nuclear power plants?

Would anyone vote for God? As you will discover in this chapter, God would have to rank, from one perspective, as the top contender for the award.

It might surprise some people, but concern for the environment is not of recent origin. Theologians have been studying the created world for centuries. In our day, however, creation theology has taken on renewed importance because environmental issues are on our hearts and minds. Creation theology is essential for a proper understanding of ecology.

But creation theology is even more important for a proper understanding of who the true and living God is. As Jesus said, "This is eternal life: that they may know you, the only true God" (John 17:3). The Bible teaches us that by studying creation, there are certain things that we can learn about God.

What did Calvin mean when he said, "The condemnation of the human race is imprinted on the heavens, the earth, and all creatures"? Let's discover the answer to this question by looking at what the Bible says about creation as a witness to the justice of God.

GOD HAS DEFILED HIS CREATION

Believe it or not, the Bible names God as the greatest defiler of the earth. What does it mean to defile something? It means to corrupt the purity and perfection of something. God himself has corrupted the purity and perfection of his creation. How so?

By the Common Curse

Think back to the period after the Fall. Genesis 3:17–19 says,

> To Adam he said, "Because you listened to your wife and ate from the tree about which I commanded you, 'You must not eat of it,' cursed is the ground because of you; through painful toil you will eat of it all the days of your life. It will produce thorns and thistles for you, and you will eat the plants of the field. By the sweat of your brow you will eat your food until you return to the ground, since from it you were taken; for dust you are and to dust you will return."

God cursed the earth because of human sin. As a result, instead of yielding only fruit, the ground now produces thorns and thistles as well. Instead of voluntarily yielding its produce to the human race, the earth now resists us. Eventually, every human being dies because of the curse. We all return to the earth from which we were taken.

Some theologians call this the "common curse" because it is an experience shared in common by all of humanity. It is experienced by every person who lives on the earth. Both the righteous and the unrighteous experience life's difficulties, the thorns and thistles of the earth. Through this curse, God defiled his originally perfect and pure creation.

By the Great Flood

Let's move ahead to Genesis 6 and the story of the Flood in Noah's day. God declared,

> I will wipe mankind, whom I have created, from the
> face of the earth—men and animals, and creatures
> that move along the ground, and birds of the air—
> for I am grieved that I have made them. . . . I am go-
> ing to bring floodwaters on the earth to destroy all
> life under the heavens, every creature that has the
> breath of life in it. Everything on earth will perish.
> (vv. 7, 17)

When you think of the Flood, you probably think of the
destruction of human beings. But the Bible says that God
brought judgment not only by destroying people, but also by
destroying animals—"every creature that has the breath of
life in it." God defiled his own creation by not only destroying human life—the epitome of God's creativity—but also
destroying "all life under the heavens."

By the Covenant Curses

Moving on still further in biblical history, we come to
God's defiling of the creation by the curses of the
covenant—the legal agreement—that he made with Israel
on Mount Sinai. In the context of that covenant, God threat-
ened to bring curses on Israel for not living in keeping with
his laws.

> You will be cursed in the city and cursed in the coun-
> try. Your basket and your kneading trough will be
> cursed. The fruit of your womb will be cursed, and
> the crops of your land, and the calves of your herds
> and the lambs of your flocks. You will be cursed
> when you come in and cursed when you go out. The
> LORD will send on you curses, confusion and rebuke
> in everything you put your hand to, until you are de-
> stroyed and come to sudden ruin because of the evil

you have done in forsaking him. The LORD will plague you with diseases until he has destroyed you from the land you are entering to possess. The LORD will strike you with wasting disease, with fever and inflammation, with scorching heat and drought, with blight and mildew, which will plague you until you perish. (Deut. 28:16–22)

These covenant curses were directed at the people of Israel, to be sure, but they also clearly included the defiling of the creation itself: scorching heat, drought, blight, mildew, and death in the flocks and herds.

By the Final Fire

Let's jump to the very end of human history, where we can find God's final defiling of creation, namely, his destruction of the creation by fire.

But the day of the Lord will come like a thief. The heavens will disappear with a roar; the elements will be destroyed by fire, and the earth and everything in it will be laid bare. Since everything will be destroyed in this way, what kind of people ought you to be? You ought to live holy and godly lives as you look forward to the day of God and speed its coming. That day will bring about *the destruction of the heavens by fire,* and the elements will melt in the heat. (2 Peter 3:10–12)

Even in evangelical literature on environmental issues, this is not a picture that is often painted: God, the defiler of creation.

Yes, God is the ultimate caretaker of creation. And that is an important truth that we must keep in mind as we think about creation, about God, and about environmental issues.

But God is also creation's defiler. We must listen to all biblical truth, not just the "nice" truth. We need the whole counsel of God if we are going to understand him and his creation, and if we wish to live in harmony with him and his creation. It is true not only that God cares for the creation, but also that he defiles his creation.

But why would the master artist defile his great masterpiece?

God Has Defiled His Creation Because of Sin

Reflect again on the biblical texts quoted above: each one documents God's defiling of creation. And each one indicates that in one way or another, God's act of defilement was his direct response to human sin.

Because of Adam's Sin

To Adam, God said, "Because you listened to your wife and ate from the tree about which I commanded you, 'You must not eat of it,' cursed is the ground because of you" (Gen. 3:17). God cursed the ground because Adam, as the representative of humanity, rebelled against the Creator.

In Adam, the whole human race rebelled against the Creator. As Paul said, "Sin entered the world through one man, and death through sin, and in this way death came to all men, *because all sinned*" (Rom. 5:12). All humans sinned. And the Creator cursed the creation because of this sin.

Because of Worldwide Sin

God defiled the creation in the days of Noah because of worldwide sin.

> When men began to increase in number on the earth
> and daughters were born to them . . . the LORD saw
> how great man's wickedness on the earth had be-
> come, and that every inclination of the thoughts of his
> heart was only evil all the time. . . . *So* the LORD said, "I
> will wipe mankind, whom I have created, from the
> face of the earth—men and animals, and creatures
> that move along the ground, and birds of the air—for
> I am grieved that I have made them." (Gen. 6:1, 5, 7)

Because of worldwide wickedness, God said he would destroy all life on the earth, not only human life, but animal life
as well. As a matter of fact, however, "Noah found favor in the
eyes of the LORD" (v. 8), and the Lord spared Noah and his
family so that his original purpose for creation might be realized. (Here we begin to get a hint of the truth that God's
"defiling" of creation is for the ultimate good of creation.)

Because of Israel's Sin

> However, if you do not obey the LORD your God and
> do not carefully follow all his commands and de-
> crees I am giving you today, all these curses will come
> upon you and overtake you. (Deut. 28:15)

As we read in the history of the people of Israel, they did
rebel, and the curses listed in Deuteronomy 28 did overtake
them. Many of the prophets wrote about these curses, but
Joel 1 is perhaps the clearest example of God's defiling the
creation in his judgment on Israel. The prophet Joel said to
his generation,

> Hear this, you elders; listen, all who live in the land.
> Has anything like this ever happened in your days or

in the days of your forefathers? . . . What the locust
swarm has left the great locusts have eaten; what the
great locusts have left the young locusts have eaten;
what the young locusts have left other locusts have
eaten. . . . The fields are ruined, the ground is dried
up; the grain is destroyed, the new wine is dried up,
the oil fails. Despair, you farmers, wail, you vine
growers; grieve for the wheat and the barley, because
the harvest of the field is destroyed. The vine is dried
up and the fig tree is withered; the pomegranate, the
palm and the apple tree—all the trees of the field—
are dried up. Surely the joy of mankind is withered
away. . . . How the cattle moan! The herds mill about
because they have no pasture; even the flocks of
sheep are suffering. To you, O LORD, I call, for fire
has devoured the open pastures and flames have
burned up all the trees of the field. Even the wild animals pant for you; the streams of water have dried
up and fire has devoured the open pastures. (Joel
1:2, 4, 10–12, 18–20)

Joel is describing the day of the Lord, the day of God's
judgment on Israel. This judgment on Israel for her
covenant disloyalty entailed a defiling of the land on which
she lived. Environmental degradation and the judgment of
God have gone together throughout the history of the Bible.

Because of Worldwide Sin Again

The day of the Lord that was experienced in Joel's own
day was a dress rehearsal for the great worldwide Day of the
Lord. Peter spoke of this day with the words, "The day of the
Lord will come like a thief" (2 Peter 3:10). Several verses earlier, Peter had said, "The present heavens and earth are reserved for fire, being kept for the day of judgment and de-

struction of ungodly men" (v. 7). Worldwide destruction will come someday because of worldwide sin.

The Bible presents a clear picture: from the time right after the first sin until the very end of history, God often manifests his judgment in the form of the destruction, degradation, and defilement of creation.

But why has he responded to human sin by defiling his creation?

GOD HAS DEFILED HIS CREATION TO TESTIFY TO HIS JUSTICE

God has defiled his creation for a purpose: so that throughout the earth there might be a testimony that the true and living God executes justice. Just as God's power and divine nature are evident throughout the creation (Rom. 1:20), so is his justice.

Everyone Knows That Death Is the Penalty for Sin

Paul teaches us that everyone knows that death is the penalty for sin.

> Furthermore, since they did not think it worthwhile to retain the knowledge of God, he gave them over to a depraved mind, to do what ought not to be done. They have become filled with every kind of wickedness, evil, greed and depravity. They are full of envy, murder, strife, deceit and malice. They are gossips, slanderers, God-haters, insolent, arrogant and boastful; they invent ways of doing evil; they disobey their parents; they are senseless, faithless, heartless, ruthless. Although *they know God's righteous decree that those who do such things deserve death,* they

not only continue to do these very things but also approve of those who practice them. (Rom. 1:28–32)

Who are those whom Paul describes as those who "know God's righteous decree that those who do such things deserve death"? He refers to absolutely everybody, including you and me. This is clear from verse 21: "For although they knew God . . ." Those who know that death is the penalty for sin are those who know God and, in the context of verses 18–21, this means absolutely everybody, for everybody knows God through his self-revelation in creation.

> The wrath of God is being revealed from heaven against *all* the godlessness and wickedness of men who suppress the truth by their wickedness, since what may be known about God is plain to them because God has made it plain to them. For since the creation of the world, God's invisible qualities—his eternal power and divine nature—have been clearly seen, being understood from what has been made, so that men are without excuse. (vv. 18–20)

Everybody is without excuse, because everybody knows that there is a true and living God whom they are to worship. Everybody—even those who claim that God does not exist—knows that failure to worship him results in "death."

But what is the "death" that everybody knows they deserve? "Death" here does not refer to the death penalty as a human judgment against crime. The proof of this is that the list of sins in verses 29–31 includes sins that did not incur the death penalty either according to Roman law or according to Old Testament law. So when Paul says, "They know God's righteous decree that those who do such things deserve death," he cannot be referring to the death penalty.

The death that they know they deserve is the death that Paul speaks of repeatedly in Romans. For example, "The wages of sin is death, but the gift of God is eternal life" (Rom. 6:23). This "death" is the opposite of eternal life. The death that everybody knows they deserve because of their sin is eternal death, although the anticipations of that death that people experience in this life are also in view.

People may not admit this truth to themselves, since they have a natural tendency to suppress the truth (see Rom. 1:18). Who likes to face the reality that he or she deserves death? So we all try to put the truth down under our heel, to crush it, to suppress it, to cover it over, to reimagine it, to do anything but admit it. But we cannot escape the truth because God has made it plain.

This Truth Is Found in Creation

How is it that everybody knows that the penalty for sin is death (eternal punishment)? Paul does not tell us explicitly in Romans 1:32. But he does hint at the answer in the previous verses, especially where he tells us implicitly that this knowledge is found in creation.

In verses 18–20, Paul teaches that through creation God has revealed himself to everybody. Because of his witness in creation, no one has an excuse for not worshiping the true and living God. The context, therefore, suggests that just as everybody knows God through the creation, so also everybody knows through the creation that death is the penalty for not obeying God and worshiping him.

God's Judgment on Creation Testifies to the Fact That He Brings Judgment on the Human Race

Why does God defile creation? When we see death and destruction in the creation around us, it is God's way of reminding us that the wages of sin is death.

Comparing two texts will clarify this point. First, look at Psalm 104, a beautiful, magnificent poem that celebrates the splendors of God's creative work. In verses 27–28, the poet portrays the Creator's kind care for his creatures:

> These all look to you
> > to give them their food at the proper time.
> When you give it to them,
> > they gather it up;
> when you open your hand,
> > they are satisfied with good things.

The poet then shocks us with stark contrast in the next verse (v. 29):

> *When you hide your face,*
> > they are terrified;
> when you take away their breath,
> > they die and return to the dust.

The hidden face of God speaks of the absence of God's favor and care. When God hides his face, animals are terrified and die.

Now consider Deuteronomy 31:17, where the focus is on God's judgment on humanity:

> On that day I will become angry with them and forsake them; *I will hide my face* from them, and they will be destroyed. Many disasters and difficulties will come upon them, and on that day they will ask, "Have not these disasters come upon us because our God is not with us?"

Do you see the parallel between these two texts? God hides his face from creation and from people. This indicates that he is angry: "On that day I will become angry with them and forsake them; I will hide my face from them." God hides his face in anger. And when he does, death results.

The language of God's judgment on humanity ("I will hide my face") echoes the language of God's treatment of the animals ("When you hide your face"). God hides his face from creation, and death follows. The same thing happens when God hides his face from people. The poet is making a point: God's treatment of creation is a testimony to his judgment on human beings.

The truth that God will bring just punishment on sinners, hiding his face from them in anger until they perish, is spread throughout creation. Every time you see an animal die, you see testimony to the justice of the true and living God. You see what one might call a preview of the final day of God's judgment, his justice and destruction.

The death and destruction that everyone sees in creation is visible testimony to the death and destruction that await sinners at the hand of a perfectly just God. The condemnation of the human race is imprinted on the creation.

Now we can understand what Calvin means when he writes, "The condemnation of the human race is imprinted on the heavens, the earth, and all creatures." Calvin is not talking about environmental degradation as a witness against us. Rather, he is talking about death and destruction as a witness to the justice of the true and living God.

There is no escape from the perfect justice of God. Yet there is escape from the death penalty. How can that be? How can there be no escape from his justice and yet escape from ultimate destruction?

GOD HAS DEFILED HIS CREATION TO TESTIFY TO HIS JUSTICE SO THAT PEOPLE MIGHT REPENT AND BE SAVED

God has defiled his creation in order to testify to his justice. He has not done this just so people will know that he is just. He has done it so that people might repent and be saved.

There is a silver lining even behind the darkest of clouds. The darkness of God's justice makes his mercy, his grace, and his power to save shine all the more brilliantly.

The Message of the Prophet Joel

The book of Joel is not long; it can be read in one sitting. Earlier we looked at Joel 1 and the bad news of God's defiling his creation. But that is only the first of three chapters. Joel 2 and 3 are filled with good news. The good news is all the more marvelous against the backdrop of the bad. Listen to just a few selections from the message of Joel:

> "Even now," declares the LORD,
>> "return to me with all your heart,
>> with fasting and weeping and mourning."
> Rend your heart
>> and not your garments.
> Return to the LORD your God,
>> for he is gracious and compassionate,
> slow to anger and abounding in love,
>> and he relents from sending calamity.
>>> (2:12–13)

> Then the LORD will be jealous for his land
>> and take pity on his people.
> The LORD will reply to them:

"I am sending you grain, new wine and oil,
　　enough to satisfy you fully;
never again will I make you
　　an object of scorn to the nations." (vv. 18–19)

Be not afraid, O land;
　　be glad and rejoice.
Surely the LORD has done great things.
Be not afraid, O wild animals,
　　for the open pastures are becoming green.
The trees are bearing their fruit;
　　the fig tree and the vine yield their riches.
Be glad, O people of Zion,
　　rejoice in the LORD your God. (vv. 21–23)

Then you will know . . .
　　that I am the LORD your God,
　　and that there is no other. (Joel 2:27)

In that day the mountains will drip new wine,
　　and the hills will flow with milk;
　　all the ravines of Judah will run with water.
A fountain will flow out of the LORD's house
　　and will water the valley of acacias. (Joel 3:18)

Their bloodguilt, which I have not pardoned,
　　I will pardon. (v. 21)

　　What a beautiful picture! What good news! There is forgiveness for repentant sinners and healing for the defiled creation. Just as our sin resulted in defilement, so our forgiveness will result in healing, not just for our souls, but for God's whole created order.

The Message of the Apostle Paul

Such good news is not unique to the prophet Joel. The apostle Paul proclaims the same good news in Romans 8:18–25, the text that Calvin was commenting on when he said, "The condemnation of the human race is imprinted on the heavens, the earth, and all creatures." Paul writes,

> I consider that our present sufferings are not worth comparing with the glory that will be revealed in us. The creation waits in eager expectation for the sons of God to be revealed. For the creation was subjected to frustration, not by its own choice, but by the will of the one who subjected it, in hope that the creation itself will be liberated from its bondage to decay and brought into the glorious freedom of the children of God.
>
> We know that the whole creation has been groaning as in the pains of childbirth right up to the present time. Not only so, but we ourselves, who have the firstfruits of the Spirit, groan inwardly as we wait eagerly for our adoption as sons, the redemption of our bodies. For in this hope we were saved. But hope that is seen is no hope at all. Who hopes for what he already has? But if we hope for what we do not yet have, we wait for it patiently.

The creation is groaning like a woman in labor. The creation is subject to frustration so that it is not all that it was created to be. The creation is in bondage to decay, because of our sin. But the creation is waiting! It is waiting for the redemption of the children of God, because our redemption will bring with it creation's liberation

from bondage. Our sin brought about creation's defilement; our redemption brings about creation's redemption.

The Creator, who has defiled the creation because of human sin, will one day redeem human sinners and the whole
of creation. How can this be? How can it be that God in his
justice can redeem?

The answer is Palm Sunday. On that day the King of creation came riding on a creature, a donkey. The King of creation rode on a creature with created palm fronds paving
the way for him. The King of creation rode triumphantly to
accomplish the redemption of sinners and the reconciliation of all things in heaven and on earth.

The answer is Good Friday. On that day the Creator was
nailed to the cross. On that day he who was equal with God
and who had not considered equality with God something
to be used for his own advantage, was hung on a tree to bear
in his own created body the penalty that we deserve. He experienced ultimate defilement at the hands of his own Father to pay the penalty for our sins.

The answer is Easter. On the day of resurrection, the ultimate defilement, death, was conquered once and for all,
not simply by the Redeemer, but by the Creator of heaven
and earth.

On Palm Sunday, Good Friday, and Easter, God manifested his power in creation to accomplish the salvation of
sinners and the reconciliation of all things in heaven and on
earth to God.

Do you understand that the world in which you live testifies to the justice of God? Do you understand that the justice of God cannot be escaped? Yet the death, defilement,
and destruction can be escaped, because the Creator bore
the just penalty in his own body on the tree.

As you rub shoulders with neighbors and coworkers who

do not know the Creator's redemptive love, there is something they do know. Everybody you talk to this week, regardless of what they tell you, regardless of what they think, knows not only that there is a true and living God whom they ought to worship, but also that the wages of their sin is death. The Word of God says so, and so does the world of God.

Although God's world tells them that the wages of their sin is death, creation does not tell them that the gift of God is eternal life through Jesus Christ our Lord. Only you can tell them that. Only you can tell them that "his anger lasts only for a moment, but his favor lasts a lifetime" (Ps. 30:5). Only you can tell them that love and joy flow from God's justice.

> Joy to the world! the Lord is come:
> Let earth receive her King;
> Let every heart prepare him room,
> And heav'n and nature sing.
>
> Joy to the earth! the Savior reigns:
> Let men their songs employ;
> While fields and floods, rocks, hills, and plains
> Repeat the sounding joy.
>
> No more let sins and sorrows grow,
> Nor thorns infest the ground;
> He comes to make his blessings flow
> Far as the curse is found.
>
> He rules the world with truth and grace,
> And makes the nations prove
> The glories of his righteousness
> And wonders of his love.

Questions for Personal Reflection or Group Discussion

1. Where do you see God's justice displayed in creation?
2. How do you respond to the apparent tension between God's love and justice in creation?
3. If the creation is going to be burned up in the end, why take care of it now?
4. How might God's justice in creation motivate you to care for the earth?

Chapter Six

Witness to the Faithfulness of God

The word of the LORD came to Jeremiah: "This is what the LORD says: 'If you can break my covenant with the day and my covenant with the night, so that day and night no longer come at their appointed time, then my covenant with David my servant—and my covenant with the Levites who are priests ministering before me—can be broken and David will no longer have a descendant to reign on his throne. I will make the descendants of David my servant and the Levites who minister before me as countless as the stars of the sky and as measureless as the sand on the seashore.'"

The word of the LORD came to Jeremiah: "Have you not noticed that these people are saying, 'The LORD has rejected the two kingdoms he chose'? So they despise my people and no longer regard them as a nation. This is what the LORD says: 'If I have not established my covenant with day and night and the fixed laws of heaven and earth, then I will reject the descendants of Jacob and David my servant and will not choose one of his sons to rule over the descendants of Abraham, Isaac and Jacob. For I will restore their fortunes and have compassion on them.'" (Jer. 33:19–26)

Has anybody ever let you down? Perhaps you were depending on someone, but that person just did not come through for you. No doubt, to one degree or another, we have all been disappointed by someone we thought we could depend on. But when push came to shove, it just did not work out. We have all been let down to varying degrees.

I remember being let down one time in particular. It was really on the more serious end of the scale. I can still picture myself standing and talking to my wife, trying to describe how I felt. I told her, "This must be how someone feels when they discover that their spouse has been unfaithful."

The more important the person, the deeper the pain is when there is unfaithfulness. Have you ever felt that God himself has let you down? If we are honest, most of us will admit that in the dark nights of the soul, we have questioned the faithfulness of God. If you have ever questioned the faithfulness of God, there may be some comfort in knowing that you were not the first person to do so, nor will you be the last.

The psalmist once questioned the faithfulness of God with these words:

> O Lord, where is your former great love,
>   which in your faithfulness you swore to David?
>   (Ps. 89:49)

Imagine these words on the lips of God's people when they were captives in Babylon, after Jerusalem, the temple, and the royal palace had all been destroyed. God had promised that David would never fail to have a son sitting on the throne, ruling over the descendants of Abraham, Isaac, and Jacob (see 2 Sam. 7:11–16 and Ps. 89:4, 28–37). But now, in captivity in Babylon, there was no Davidic king and no throne. There were only the haunting words of Psalm 89:49.

Questioning God's faithfulness is not new. In the Psalms you will find an articulation of your own burning questions. For people asking such soul-searching questions, the book of Jeremiah was written.

In a sense, this chapter is the most important chapter in the book. For what good is God's power if we cannot depend on him to use it faithfully for our good, day after day? What good is God's love, if we cannot depend on him to be faithful in his love for us, day after day after day? What good is it to know that God is just if we cannot depend on him to be faithful in his justice?

First, let's consider *how* God displays his faithfulness in creation. Then we will be in a position to discover *why* he does so.

GOD DISPLAYS HIS FAITHFULNESS IN CREATION

God displays his faithfulness in creation in many ways. I will only touch upon the two ways that Jeremiah mentions: the regularity of the sun and the moon, and the regularity of the oceans.

In the Regularity of the Sun and the Moon

A Regularity Established at Creation. The regularity of the sun and the moon was established by God when he created the universe.

> This is what the LORD says,
> he who appoints the sun
> to shine by day,
> who decrees the moon and stars
> to shine by night,

who stirs up the sea
so that its waves roar—
the LORD Almighty is his name. (Jer. 31:35)

Jeremiah is alluding to Genesis 1:14, where God says, "Let there be lights in the expanse of the sky to separate the day from the night, and let them serve as signs to mark seasons and days and years." Jeremiah is alluding to the beginning, when God created the sun, the moon, and the stars for marking seasons, days, and years and for giving light to the earth.

The Regularity of the Sun. Genesis 1:17 says of the sun, the moon, and the stars that "God set them in the expanse of the sky to give light on the earth." And that is exactly what the sun has been doing ever since. It has been giving light on the earth. The sun has been doing just that for as long as it has been in existence.

Astronomers tells us that the brightness of the sun has not changed since the day of its birth. It's a star that has been shining at the same brilliance from its beginning. Many astronomers, including astronomers who believe in the Bible, estimate the age of the sun to be about 4.5 billion years. Imagine the sun, shining steadily, day after day, for 4.5 billion years! The sun provides an extraordinary testimony to the faithfulness of God in maintaining his creation.

Since you became a Christian, have you been faithful to read your Bible and pray every day? Probably not one of us has been that faithful in our Scripture reading and prayer, and some of us have only been Christians for a few years. When we compare our faithfulness in devotions to God's faithfulness in maintaining the sun, the sun becomes a stellar witness to the faithfulness of God. Can you bank on the sun coming up tomorrow? Sure you can. Even when it's cloudy, we know that the sun is still shining.

I remember the very first time I flew in an airplane. I was

in my early twenties and was flying from Philadelphia to Madison, Wisconsin. I was delayed in Chicago because of bad weather. We had to circle above the airport for what seemed like hours before we were finally permitted to land. Then we were not allowed to take off because the airport in Madison was closed. When we were finally cleared for take-off from Chicago and then broke through the clouds, what a beautiful day was up above! If you've flown much, you too have had that experience. The sun was shining in all of its brilliance, though obscured from view on the ground. Even on the darkest day, the dependability of the sun is a testimony to the faithfulness of God.

The Regularity of the Moon. Jeremiah also mentions the regularity of the moon. The moon revolves around the earth with great regularity: once every 27 days, 7 hours, 43 minutes, and 11.5 seconds.

Or think about the phases of the moon. At the new moon, you cannot see the moon because it is between the sun and the earth, so the moon's face is not illuminated by the sun. Then there is the first quarter, when the right half of the moon is illuminated. Full moon is when the earth is between the moon and the sun, so that the whole face is illuminated. Then comes the third quarter, when the left half is illuminated before it wanes into the new moon. The moon goes through its phases with great regularity every 29 days, 12 hours, 44 minutes, and 2.8 seconds.

Ancient Israelites had neither daily planners nor calendar watches. How did they tell when one month ended and the next month began? They watched the phases of the moon. These phases are so regular that the ancients based their calendars on them (see Num. 28:14 and Isa. 66:23).

A Regularity Established as a Covenant. The regularity of the sun and the moon was established at creation as a covenant.

(A covenant is a relationship with responsibilities or obligations attached to it.) God established a covenant relationship with creation in the beginning, as he says through Jeremiah,

> This is what the LORD says:
> "If you can break *my covenant with the day and my covenant with the night,* so that day and night no longer come at their appointed time" . . . "If I have not established *my covenant with day and night* and the fixed laws of heaven and earth . . ." (Jer. 33:20, 25)

The whole of creation is in a covenant relationship with God. Creation is under obligation to the Creator. The sun and the moon shine day after day because it is their covenantal obligation to do so.

This is why verse 25 refers to "the fixed laws of heaven." Just as God has given his people covenantal obligations in the Ten Commandments, so God has given covenantal obligations to the sun and moon. God did not give them a law that says, "Do not commit adultery," but he did give them a law that says, "Shine every day." He obligated the moon to go around the earth day after day and to go through its phases regularly. This covenantal relationship was established by God with the creation at the time of creation.

This covenant was renewed after the Flood. The Flood seemed to turn the whole creation upside down and to obliterate God's order. But after the Flood, God said,

> As long as the earth endures,
> seedtime and harvest,
> cold and heat,
> summer and winter,
> day and night
> will never cease. (Gen. 8:22)

The point of this text can be summarized with one word: faithfulness. As long as the earth endures, God will faithfully maintain the regularity of creation. This means that this regularity was established for all time.

A Regularity Established for All Time. Jeremiah makes the point that it is utterly unthinkable that the sun would stop shining. It is utterly unthinkable that the moon would quit orbiting the earth or going through its phases. That is utterly unthinkable because God established this regularity at creation as a covenant for all time.

In the Regularity of the Oceans

Jeremiah draws our attention not only to the sun and the moon, but also to the oceans, by referring to God as the one "who stirs up the sea so that its waves roar" (Jer. 31:35).

An Ordinary Regularity. Think for a moment about the regularity of the waves. Whenever people go to the beach, they take for granted that the waves will just keep rolling in and lapping onto the shore.

Or consider the tides. High tide is the result of the gravitational force of the moon, and to a lesser degree the sun, exerted on the ocean. Whenever the moon is directly above the ocean, it draws all of that water upward, making the tide high. Oceanographers call this the direct tide. When the moon is directly opposite the ocean, the same force is at work, but this is called the opposite tide. For these reasons, there are two high tides each day. The time of the high tide can be predicted with great accuracy. The great regularity in the waves and the tides is a testimony to the faithfulness of God.

A Divine Regularity. What we experience as a quite ordinary regularity in the ocean's waves and tides is at the same time a divine regularity. Jeremiah says that God is the one "who stirs up the sea so that its waves roar" (Jer. 31:35).

Why is there such amazing regularity in the ocean? Why is there such regularity in the sun and the moon? It's not the result of an accidental convergence of forces through purely natural processes. It's because there is a true and living God, the Creator of heaven and earth, who not only spoke his word at the beginning and said, "Let there be light" and "Let the water under the sky be gathered to one place" (Gen. 1:3, 9), but also day by day continues to speak his sustaining word to maintain the regularity of the creation (Heb. 1:3).

Why does the sun come up faithfully? Why does the moon orbit faithfully? Why do the waves crash on the shore faithfully? Why do the tides ebb and flow faithfully? Because God is ever faithful to his creation. All of this regularity in creation, and much, much more, is testimony to the faithfulness of the Creator.

So what is the point? Let's see what the point was for Jeremiah, and what it should be for us.

A WITNESS TO HIS FAITHFULNESS TO HIS PROMISES

God displays his faithfulness in creation as a witness to his faithfulness to his promises. That God is faithful to his promises is what the people in exile in Jeremiah's day needed to know. Since their circumstances seemed to cry out, "God is not faithful," they needed assurance that God was ever faithful to his promises.

God's Promises Given

God has given many promises, but here we will focus on

the promises that Jeremiah has in view: those given to Abraham and to David.

Promises Given to Abraham.

> "Only if these decrees vanish from my sight,"
>   declares the LORD,
> "will the descendants of Israel ever cease
>   to be a nation before me." (Jer. 31:36)

> This is what the LORD says: "If I have not established my covenant with day and night and the fixed laws of heaven and earth, then I will reject the descendants of Jacob and David my servant and will not choose one of his sons to rule over the descendants of Abraham, Isaac and Jacob. For I will restore their fortunes and have compassion on them." (Jer. 33:25–26)

Jeremiah is alluding to Genesis 17:4–7, where God says,

> As for me, this is my covenant with you: You will be the father of many nations. No longer will you be called Abram; your name will be Abraham, for I have made you a father of many nations. I will make you very fruitful; I will make nations of you, and kings will come from you. I will establish my covenant as an everlasting covenant between me and you and your descendants after you for the generations to come, to be your God and the God of your descendants after you.

Two key elements in the promises made to Abraham are of interest to us. First, God promised that Abraham and his descendants would always be the people of God. The "descendants of Abraham" in view are not simply the nation of Israel, because Abraham would eventually be the "father of many nations." The children of Abraham would consist of both Jews and Gentiles (see Gal. 3:26–29). Second, God promised that kings would come from Abraham.

God's people in exile were forced to question God's faithfulness to his promise that Abraham's descendants would always be God's people and that he would always be their God. Earlier, in Jeremiah 3:8, we read,

> I gave faithless Israel her certificate of divorce and sent her away because of all her adulteries. Yet I saw that her unfaithful sister Judah had no fear; she also went out and committed adultery.

Jeremiah described the exile of the northern tribes of Israel in terms of God divorcing his wife because of her adulterous idolatry. The southern tribe of Judah, now in exile, must have asked, "What does Jeremiah 3:8 mean for us? Does it not mean that we, too, have been divorced by God because of our adulterous idolatry?" The words of Hosea 1:9 must have reinforced an affirmative answer to these questions: "Then the LORD said, 'Call him Lo-Ammi, for you are not my people, and I am not your God.'" Thus, the captivity forced God's people to question the faithfulness of God to the promise he had made to Abraham.

> I will establish my covenant as an everlasting covenant between me and you and your descendants after you for the generations to come, to be your God and the God of your descendants after you. (Gen. 17:7)

Then there was the promise that kings would come from Abraham, presumably to rule over Abraham's descendants. This promise was fulfilled on one level when God made the covenant of kingship with David, which leads us to consider that covenant, even as Jeremiah referred both to the covenant promises given to Abraham and to those given to David.

Promises Given to David. God had promised Abraham that kings would come from him. David was the fulfillment of that promise. But when God made David king, God gave him additional promises. God promised David that he would never fail to have a son sitting on the throne and ruling over the people of God.

> But my love will never be taken away from him, as I took it away from Saul, whom I removed from before you. (2 Sam. 7:15)

> Once for all, I have sworn by my holiness—
>   and I will not lie to David—
> that his line will continue forever. (Ps. 89:35–36)

But God's people were now in captivity in Babylon. There was no throne; the Babylonians had destroyed it. No son of David was reigning over the people. It looked as if God had not been faithful to his promises. Jeremiah's job was to persuade the people in captivity that God was, in fact, not unfaithful, but that he is ever faithful.

How could he succeed, when circumstances seemed so clearly to contradict the promises of God? How could he persuade them of the faithfulness of God? What kind of argument could he offer? What kind of testimony could he bring forth? *The testimony of creation!*

Now you can see what Jeremiah was doing. As the people questioned the faithfulness of God to the promises he had made to Abraham and David, God said,

> Only if these decrees vanish from my sight . . . will the descendants of Israel ever cease to be a nation before me. (Jer. 31:36)

> If you can break my covenant with the day and my covenant with the night, so that day and night no longer come at their appointed time, then my covenant with David my servant—and my covenant with the Levites who are priests ministering before me—can be broken and David will no longer have a descendant to reign on his throne. (Jer. 33:20–21)

> If I have not established my covenant with day and night and the fixed laws of heaven and earth, then I will reject the descendants of Jacob and David my servant and will not choose one of his sons to rule over the descendants of Abraham, Isaac and Jacob. For I will restore their fortunes and have compassion on them. (vv. 25–26)

Do you want evidence that God is forever faithful? Look at the creation. See there the display of his great faithfulness.

> Once for all, I have sworn by my holiness—
>   and I will not lie to David—
> that his line will continue forever
>   and his throne endure before me *like the sun;*
> it will be established forever *like the moon,*
>   *the faithful witness in the sky.* (Ps. 89:35–37)

Was this just nice rhetoric, or did God come through and fulfill the promises given to Abraham and David?

God's Promises Fulfilled

In Christ. All of God's promises are fulfilled in Christ (2 Cor. 1:20). Christ is the son whom God promised to Abraham and to David. Matthew begins his gospel with these words: "A record of the genealogy of Jesus Christ the son of David, the son of Abraham" (Matt. 1:1). The first thing we are told about Jesus is that he was "the son of David, the son of Abraham." God was faithful. He did send the promised son: he sent the Lord Jesus Christ, a descendant of both Abraham and David.

The Hebrew word we translate as "descendants" in Genesis 17:8 is the word often translated "seed." Listen to what Paul says in Galatians 3:16, 19:

> The promises were spoken to Abraham and to his *seed.* The Scripture does not say "and to *seeds,*" meaning many people, but "and to your *seed,*" meaning one person, who is *Christ. . . .* What, then, was the purpose of the law? It was added because of transgressions until the *Seed* to whom the promise referred had come.

To whom did the promise refer when God said that Abraham would have a seed? The promise referred to Christ. To whom did the promise refer when God said that David would never fail to have a son sitting on the throne? The promise referred to Christ. The promises given to Abraham and David were fulfilled in Christ.

Christ is not only the descendant of Abraham and the

son of David, but also the mediator of the new covenant. Consider the context of Jeremiah 31–33:

> "The time is coming," declares the LORD, "when I will make a *new covenant* with the house of Israel and with the house of Judah." (Jer. 31:31)

When and where was this new covenant inaugurated? Jesus tells us in the words of Luke 22:20: "In the same way, after the supper he took the cup, saying, 'This cup is the *new covenant* in my blood, which is poured out for you.'"

How could God ever be faithful to that adulterous generation in captivity? How can God ever be faithful to you and me, in our faithlessness and sin? Through Jesus Christ! Jesus was the faithful seed of Abraham, the faithful son of David, the faithful king reigning over us, the faithful priest atoning for our sin, and the faithful prophet teaching in word and deed the utter faithfulness of God.

Like God's people in captivity, we do not deserve the least bit of God's faithfulness. Well, yes we do. We do deserve for God to be utterly faithful in his justice, and to consign us to hell forever. But the slightest blessing we have received from his hand, we have forfeited by our sin. So our only hope of experiencing the faithfulness of God in salvation is provided by the fact that he has been faithful to send his Son, the seed of Abraham, the son of David, the Savior of the World.

In the Church. But these promises are fulfilled, not only in Christ, but also in the church. Through union with Christ, the church is also the "seed" of Abraham. God had promised Abraham that he would be the father of many nations, not just the father of Jews. The church, made up of

Jews and Gentiles, is now the seed of Abraham. This is what Paul says in Galatians 3:26–29:

> You are all sons of God through faith in Christ Jesus, for all of you who were baptized into Christ have clothed yourselves with Christ. There is neither Jew nor Greek, slave nor free, male nor female, for you are all one in Christ Jesus. If you belong to Christ, then you are Abraham's seed, and heirs according to the promise.

Who will inherit all the promises made to Abraham? The determining factor is not ethnic connection, but connection to Christ. "If you belong to Christ, then you are Abraham's seed, and heirs according to the promise."

If you are not connected to Christ by God's grace through faith, then you are not an heir of the promise. But God is faithful to save all those who call on him. In observing the sun coming up or the moon orbiting the earth, know that God will be faithful to save all who bow to King Jesus, who listen to his prophetic word, who trust in his priestly sacrifice for sin. So come and place your life under him, embrace him, and begin to participate in all of the blessings of the covenant that God has for those who are united to Christ.

Will God be faithful to give you the grace you need to endure trials? Will God be faithful to deliver you from the abuse you receive at the hands of others? Will God be faithful to give you the strength you need to overcome the sin that entangles you? Will God be faithful to forgive you yet one more time when you fail to overcome that sin? Will God be faithful to complete the salvation that he has begun in you? Will God be faithful to accept you when you question his faithfulness?

The Lord says that just as you cannot break his covenant with the day and his covenant with the night so that day and night no longer come at their appointed time, so also he will never fail to be faithful to you and will never reject you, and will have compassion on you in Jesus Christ.

> Once for all, I have sworn by my holiness—
> and I will not lie to David—
> that his line will continue forever
> and his throne endure before me like the sun;
> it will be established forever like the moon,
> the faithful witness in the sky. (Ps. 89:35–37)

Before concluding this chapter, pause to meditate on the faithfulness of God by using the words of that well-known hymn by Thomas O. Chisholm, "Great Is Thy Faithfulness":

> Great is thy faithfulness, O God my Father;
> There is no shadow of turning with thee;
> Thou changest not, thy compassions, they fail not;
> As thou hast been thou forever wilt be.
>
> Summer and winter and springtime and harvest,
> Sun, moon, and stars in their courses above,
> Join with all nature in manifold witness
> To thy great faithfulness, mercy, and love.
>
> Pardon for sin and a peace that endureth,
> Thine own dear presence to cheer and to guide,
> Strength for today and bright hope for tomorrow,
> Blessings all mine, with ten thousand beside!
>
> Great is thy faithfulness! Great is thy faithfulness!
> Morning by morning new mercies I see:

All I have needed thy hand hath provided—
Great is thy faithfulness, Lord, unto me!

QUESTIONS FOR PERSONAL REFLECTION OR GROUP DISCUSSION

1. In what particular ways do you experience God's faithfulness in nature?
2. Do you ever doubt that God is faithful? How might the creation strengthen your faith in the faithfulness of God?
3. Is there a particular area in your life where God is calling you to grow in faithfulness? How can the witness to God's faithfulness in creation motivate you to be more faithful?